PERSPECTIVES ON

Civil Unrest in the 1960s

Riots and Their Aftermath

WIL MARA

mc **Marshall Cavendish**
Benchmark
New York

Marshall Cavendish Benchmark
99 White Plains Road
Tarrytown, NY 10591-5502
www.marshallcavendish.us

Expert Reader: Professor Michael Flamm, Department of History, Ohio Wesleyan
University, Delaware, Ohio

Library of Congress Cataloging-in-Publication Data

Mara, Wil
Civil unrest in the 1960s : riots and their aftermath / by Wil Mara.
p. cm. — (Perspectives on)
Includes bibliographical references and index.
Summary: "Provides comprehensive information on civil unrest during the 1960s
and the factors that drove these events"—Provided by publisher.
ISBN 978-0-7614-4025-3
1. United States—Social conditions—1960–1980. 2. United States—Politics and
government—1945–1989. 3. Riots—United States—History—20th century. 4.
United States—Race relations—History—20th century. I. Title.
HN59.M285 2009
303.6'23097309046—dc22
2008024673

Editor: Christine Florie
Publisher: Michelle Bisson
Art Director: Anahid Hamparian
Series Designer: Sonia Chaghatzbanian

Photo research by Marybeth Kavanagh

Cover photo by Bettmann/Corbis

The photographs in this book are used by permission and through the courtesy of:
Bettmann/*Corbis*: 2, 52, 55, 65, 69, 76, 97; New York Times Co./*Getty Images*: 12, 104;
Mary Evans Picture Library/*The Image Works*: 18; George Silk/Time Life Pictures/
Getty Images: 23; Topham/*The Image Works*: 25, 61; Kyoichi Sawada/Bettmann/*Corbis*:
31; Wally McNamee/*Corbis*: 34; JP Laffont/Sygma/*Corbis*: 39; Charles Gatewood/
The Image Works: 44; Lee Balterman/Time Life Pictures/*Getty Images*: 48; Bentley
Archive/Popperfoto/*Getty Images*: 75; Art Shay/Time Life Pictures/*Getty Images*: 91;
Vernon Merritt III/Time Life Pictures/*Getty Images*: 101

Printed in Malaysia
1 3 5 6 4 2

Contents

Introduction

THE ACT OF RIOTING MAY SEEM CONTEMPTIBLE to many. It may seem the work of people with little or no regard for the safety of others or the value of their property. People who riot are often considered unprincipled, out of control, and animalistic in their behavior. Rioting is often looked on as an irrational act committed by irrational individuals, most of whom should be locked up for giving in to that primal impulse.

But if you speak with those who have actually participated in a riot, you may encounter a very different viewpoint. Many will speak self-righteously, insisting that their actions were not unprincipled, but in fact a response to serious injustices — wrongs that had been allowed to grow so large that they left people of goodwill no choice but to make a statement through anger and violence.

Accordingly, there is more than one perspective concerning the civil unrest that characterized much of the 1960s. It was a decade of turmoil, a decade of uncertainty, a decade of redefining roles, and yes, occasionally a decade of unspeakable violence. Issues that had rarely been discussed in public forums were suddenly ripped from their hiding places and thrust into the limelight. People who never had a voice in America's social debate wanted to be heard. And those who had gotten used to manning the controls found their power threatened for the very first time. It was an age rife with discord and ready for change — change that often came at a very high price.

This book is partially about the civil unrest of that decade. But in a broader sense it is also about the unique factors that drove these events. It is furthermore an attempt to present all sides of the issues that caused so much friction — and to make you consider just how much noise from that era still echoes in American society today. As a result you will be able to form your own opinion. In the same way that industrialization set the tone from the beginning of the twentieth century to the post–World War II era, so the 1960s set much of the tone of the present. Do you know of a woman who holds a position of great importance in a company? Do you know of a black man who earns a six-figure salary? Do you know why some people are suspicious and mistrustful of their political leaders? These aspects of our culture didn't *always* exist.

Let's take a trip back in time.

PART I: ANGER

To many, America after World War II was like a paradise. Those who had suffered during the harsh Depression years, which followed the stock market crash of 1929, were delighted when the nation was reenergized by thousands of new job opportunities, generous government programs, and a robust economy. In the late 1940s and throughout the 1950s, millions of people who had been unable to find work suddenly had secure positions with solid companies, handsome salaries, and beautiful homes—and they represented a growing section of society known as the middle class. Before these boom years barely one-third of Americans could say they were in this category—but after World War II that number doubled. People had cash in their pockets, and there were plenty of exciting ways to spend it—on new homes, new cars, new appliances, new furniture. Many sent their children to college, took vacations to exotic locales, and ate at the finest restaurants. There was often money left over for personal saving and investment. In short, most Americans had more than ever before.

But not everyone benefited from this period of unparalleled prosperity. Some seemed to be left out, and it didn't take long for them to begin wondering if they were being purposely excluded. Many ethnic minority groups, for example, were unable to dip their cups into the swelling stream of newfound wealth and opportunity. Blacks, in particular—who had been treated as second-class citizens for centuries—were increasingly frustrated by countless barriers that separated them from the good life they saw depicted in the media. In many towns and cities they were reminded daily of the subordinate role they had been assigned—department stores in which they could not shop, restaurants in which they could not eat, and schools in which they could not learn. James Roberson, a resident of Birmingham, Alabama, remembers, "The green sign on the Birmingham city buses was one of the most powerful in the city. . . . On one side of the board it said, 'Colored [people] do not sit beyond this board.' The bus driver had the authority to move that green board in any direction he wanted to at any time." Women, too, felt they were being denied opportunities because of the expectation that they should either stay at home and care for their families or, if they did have a job, should accept pay that was considerably less than that of men—and often for the same work.

As the 1950s wore on, other people joined blacks and women in the dissatisfied population. Young men and women of college age, for example, who wanted a greater voice in the governing of America, felt that their views were being dismissed as the product of inexperience and ignorance. "Campuses in the 1950s were not political places," wrote William S. McConnell in *The Counterculture Movement of the 1960s*. "College administrators discouraged students from exploring serious politics." Other people were alarmed by the horrid treatment of the natural environment, which was being damaged—often irreversibly—by the explosive growth of the human population and by a lack of concern by some big businesses.

As the 1950s gave way to the 1960s, the collective voice of rebellion ceased being a whisper and began building to a sustained roar. By the middle of the decade an unpopular overseas war was forced upon America by its leaders. As this war went from bad to worse, the tension evolved into anger. Those who were outraged demanded action, and those who had the power to act ignored them. By early 1968 more than half a million troops had been committed, nearly 23,000 American deaths had occurred, and the fight was costing about $1 billion a month. The anger evolved yet again, and those who wanted change came to the conclusion that they had no choice but to take matters into their own hands. If the people running the country would not help them, then they would help themselves.

And so began the storm that forever changed a nation.

One

Racism in America

IMAGINE WALKING DOWN THE SIDEWALK on a chilly night. You come to the window of an elegant restaurant—the tables are covered with white linen, the crystal and silverware sparkle in the candlelight. It looks warm inside, and the customers seem comfortable and happy. Waiters and waitresses bring more food and drink; there seems to be an endless supply. You would love nothing more than to go inside and have a hot meal. You have money in your pocket, money that's just as good as anyone else's.

But then you see the sign by the front door—*Whites Only*. You're not white; you're black. And in this time and place, that means you can't eat here. You're considered second-rate, "less" than the people inside. It hurts to think about this. It hurts in every way that something can hurt. You know you aren't really less than they are, but you have no chance to prove it. In this society you're judged first by your color—something you were born with and had no control over.

This is racism.

Racism has played a major role in U.S. history, leading to much of the civil unrest in the 1960s. In 1950 this theater had a segregated entrance.

Slavery

Racism in America, applied specifically against black people, essentially began with the horrendous practice of slavery. In simple terms slavery is the ownership of one human being by another, usually for the purpose of forcing someone to perform tasks that he or she did not choose to do, and without pay.

Slavery in colonial America began in the early 1600s and was practiced in the United States until the mid-1800s. Most slave owners were farmers who wanted to put workers in their fields for little or no money. This was necessary, the farmers claimed, to keep their costs down so they could offer their products at a good price. Three categories of persons performed forced labor at the beginning of this period — American Indians, indentured servants, and Africans. Beginning toward the end of the 1600s millions of people born and raised on the continent of Africa were taken from their villages and families, herded onto overcrowded ships, and transported across the Atlantic Ocean to England and North America. They were then sold to the highest bidders as part of a growing business known as the slave trade.

In Colonial and pre-Emancipation America, the life that followed was usually one of backbreaking labor. Slaves rose early, put in long hours, and often collapsed from exhaustion at the end of the day. They usually received no money for their labor. Instead, they were given a small cabin at the far end of their owner's property (among a cluster of cabins inhabited by other slaves), food, and clothing. If they were lucky, their owner would provide medical care as needed. They might also be promised their freedom one day — but only after spending the best years of their lives making their owners rich. There were no laws to protect slaves, no laws that recognized their basic rights. Many slaves were treated with unspeakable cruelty and lived out their days in utter hopelessness.

In spite of all this, some people tried to cast slavery in a positive light. In 1855 William John Grayson wrote, "The slave . . . owes his labour to his master. Slavery . . . ensures homes, food and clothing for all. It permits no idleness, and it provides for sickness, infancy and old age. It allows no tramping or skulking, and it knows no pauperism."

Emancipation

Not everyone in America approved of slavery. In the northern states and in England, for example, many people were against it, and slavery was eventually outlawed in those places. By 1830 slavery in America was legal only in the southern states, which caused tremendous tension between the South and the North. Southern slaveholders continued to maintain that the practice was necessary for the survival of the farming industry—the South, which had thousands of farms, could not sustain itself without cheap labor.

In 1860 Abraham Lincoln became president of the United States. Raised in the northern state of Illinois, Lincoln was determined to abolish slavery. Like many others, he found it an abomination against the laws of God. His election further increased the tension between the slave states and the free states, and it sparked the start of the Civil War. On January 1, 1863, as the war raged on, he issued the second and final part of the historic Emancipation Proclamation, granting freedom to more than 3 million slaves. Plenty of people opposed this move, but Lincoln held his ground. "You dislike the emancipation proclamation; and, perhaps, would have it retracted. You say it is unconstitutional — I think differently," he wrote some months after the Emancipation Proclamation was issued. The final blow to slavery was the ratification of the Thirteenth Amendment to the U.S. Constitution, which abolished it forever.

Free . . . but Hardly Equal

After the Civil War the nation went through a rebuilding period known as Reconstruction. The government tried to help former slaves start a new and better life. Some were given jobs, money, and tracts of land on which to grow and sell their own crops. New laws were written to protect such basic rights as the right to vote in public elections, and indeed, the Reconstruction period saw the election of black mayors, congressmen, and even senators.

Progress, however, wasn't very widespread, for in the southern states the effort to keep blacks from enjoying the benefits of a free society was as strong as ever. Former slaveholders were bitter over the loss of their "property," and former Confederates, slaveholders and nonslaveholders alike, were equally bitter over the loss of the war. Citizens refused to buy goods from black farmers, forcing them to sell their land and go back to working on farms owned by whites, and groups known as white supremacists terrorized black families. Blacks were often savagely beaten and sometimes killed. And then there was segregation — the practice of keeping blacks separated from whites except in a service capacity. Southern states wrote laws forbidding blacks from interacting with whites: they couldn't go to the same schools, play in the same parks, or sit in the same sections on buses. A black man could get in trouble for speaking to a white girl.

The Emancipation Proclamation

Many people don't realize that the Emancipation Proclamation didn't actually end slavery—it only forbade it in certain areas. The proclamation consisted of not one but two executive orders from President Lincoln. The first, issued on September 22, 1862, granted freedom to all slaves living in the Confederate States of America. The second executive order, issued on January 1, 1863, specified which states were affected. Slavery wasn't outlawed everywhere in America until December 6, 1865, with the ratification of the Thirteenth Amendment.

Frustrated and out of patience, many blacks moved away. They went north or to the developing western states. Some returned to Africa. But most were stuck in the South because they didn't have the means to leave. Angry citizens, both black and white, began speaking out. Black-only schools were built, giving many black children a chance at a decent education. Pro-black organizations formed for the first time, including, in 1909, the National Association for the Advancement of Colored People (NAACP)—which still has tremendous influence today. At last blacks, with the help of sympathetic whites, were beginning to gain some power.

The mission of the NAACP is to "ensure a society in which all individuals have equal rights and there is no racial hatred or racial discrimination." This is their New York office in 1933.

The Depression and the New Deal

Not long after World War I America (and, in fact, most of the world) experienced one of the worst economic disasters in human history—the Great Depression. Banks closed, investments became worthless, and millions of dollars were lost in property and savings. While white people were hit hard, blacks were hit harder. Companies that had to release a percentage of their employees often laid off their black workers first. By the mid-1930s more than two-thirds of the adult black population in America was unable to earn a living. Most had to rely on government handouts to survive.

One attempt to ease this suffering came in the form of the New Deal program initiated by President Franklin D. Roosevelt. Roosevelt consulted with hundreds of black leaders to learn more about the problems blacks were facing and to discuss ideas about how best to solve them. Through New Deal programs thousands of blacks were given government jobs, loans and grants, and inexpensive homes. These were steps in the right direction, and many blacks became supporters of the Democratic Party as a result.

Taking the Battle to the Courts

During the 1930s many black leaders decided to use the American court system to fight segregation and other forms of discrimination. There were more black lawyers than ever before, not to mention whites in the legal profession who were compassionate toward the black struggle. It was time to use the law to favor victims of racial injustice.

Lawyers attacked racial discrimination on all fronts, forcing schools and businesses to give black citizens the same treatment as whites. Threats of boycotts or lawsuits often worked in the short term, but a broader, more permanent step was needed—and it came in 1954 with the landmark case known as *Brown v. Board of Education of Topeka*. A unanimous decision by the U.S. Supreme Court established that segregation by race in the public schools was in violation of the Constitution, specifically the equal protection clause of the Fourteenth Amendment.

For decades most of America had supported the practice of racial segregation. Even in the northern states, where blacks had considerably more respect and opportunities, there were black churches and white churches, black schools and white schools, and so on. For the people who didn't like blacks, this seemed like a reasonable compromise—until many black people began to complain that their children's schools were nowhere near as good as those of whites.' Black schools, for example, were often in need of repair and short on quality textbooks, whereas the white schools usually had everything they needed. And black neighborhoods rarely received the same funding as white neighborhoods for government programs. The idea of "separate but equal" was the foundation on which segregation rested—but there was almost no true equality involved.

Brown v. Board of Education was the first major blow to the "separate but equal" policy. Thereafter, nothing would be the same—everyone sympathetic to the black fight for equality had a legal precedent to build upon. Laws based on the "separate but equal" policy were now unconstitutional.

From the liberal standpoint the *Brown* decision was an overwhelming victory. The *Chicago Defender*, a major black newspaper, went so far as to call it the "second emancipation proclamation." But for conservatives, it meant something

Plessy v. Ferguson and the "Separate but Equal" Doctrine

In 1896 the U.S. Supreme Court heard *Plessy v. Ferguson*, in which Homer Plessy, who was one-eighth black, argued that his constitutional rights had been violated when he was asked to remove himself from a "whites-only" railroad car and sit in a car designated for blacks. The Court ruled against Plessy, setting a powerful legal precedent in support of the "separate but equal" policy that meant blacks would be obliged to use public and commercial facilities that were separate from—but theoretically equal to—those available to whites. For example, they would have their own schools, their own restaurants, and so on. However, these facilities were often less than equal in terms of quality or funding. But it wasn't until the *Brown v. Board of Education* decision, handed down in 1954, that the racist policies supported by the *Plessy* ruling were eliminated.

very different, especially in the South, where conservatives believed progress toward black equality was already being made, so there was no need for the Supreme Court to interfere. The result was increased resentment toward southern blacks, making matters worse instead of better. Many also believed that the decision represented federal intrusion upon states' rights, as guaranteed by the Tenth Amendment to the Constitution. There was even belief among some whites that blacks were a naturally inferior race and therefore *needed* to be ruled by whites, and that the power given to blacks through the *Brown* decision was more than they were ready for.

The Civil Rights Movement

In spite of the conservative outcry, blacks in America put a big dent in repealing racist policies thanks to the potential unleashed by the *Brown* decision—but they knew they still faced enormous hurdles. One, of course, was achieving enforcement of this legal victory. Making discrimination against blacks a thing of the past was going to be tough.

In the South, for example, many school officials, in spite of the ruling in *Brown*, refused to allow blacks to enroll. In other words, they simply ignored the Supreme Court. For example, in Little Rock, Arkansas, in 1957, nine black students who were supposed to begin attending classes at Central High School were blocked by local and state officials. In response, President Dwight D. Eisenhower sent the National Guard to make certain the children could safely enter their classrooms.

Segregation continued to exist in many other places as well—restaurants, supermarkets, playgrounds, and all forms

The Little Rock Nine enter Central High School under the protection of the 101st Airborne Command.

of public transportation. On December 1, 1955, however, one person decided to take a stand. Rosa Parks, a forty-two-year-old black woman who belonged to the NAACP in Montgomery, Alabama, was told to give her seat on a bus to a white man. She refused, and she was promptly arrested. In response to this, a young Baptist minister named Martin Luther King Jr. organized a boycott of the local transit system—all blacks, he said, should abstain from using buses throughout the city. The strategy worked, as more than 90 percent of black bus riders honored the request. The drop in fares was a financial disaster for the bus companies, and a court order was eventually issued, forcing them to desegregate their vehicles.

The Montgomery bus boycott turned King into a nationally recognized figure. He was an intelligent and passionate young man with amazing speaking skills, and he was soon regarded as the new leader of the civil rights movement. He gained tremendous popularity through his peaceful, nonviolent approach to fighting racism—he would organize other boycotts, sit-ins, and protest marches while giving inspiring speeches all around the country (mostly in the South). Fred Taylor, who was just thirteen and a resident of Montgomery during this period remembers:

> At the time the boycott began, all these news
> reporters started following my pastor and
> Dr. King around. Something I guess happened
> to me, particularly as I began to listen to
> Dr. King's speeches. I can remember going
> to mass meetings during the boycott and
> hearing him speak. You know the mastery of
> the English language that Dr. King had. I can
> remember the euphoria.

King soon had hundreds of thousands of followers, all of whom felt they had finally found the man who could make the changes that needed making.

The black leader described his increasingly popular protest strategy of nonviolent civil disobedience as a moral imperative when a majority imposed unjust laws upon a minority denied basic political rights. But those of

Throngs of followers gather to listen to the inspirational message of Dr. Martin Luther King Jr. in Montgomery, Alabama.

a conservative viewpoint thought very differently. They felt that order must be maintained regardless of protestors' motivation and that laws were what kept a nation from descending into chaos. They were also troubled by King's practice of gathering large groups of peaceful supporters, for they feared the creation of a "mob mentality." This, they felt, was a step toward anarchy—a society lacking in government and rule of law. Nevertheless, King continued drawing such crowds, giving speeches, and staging peaceful protests as his influence grew.

Then came April 4, 1968—the day he was assassinated.

Two

The War in Vietnam

PRIOR TO THE 1960s, IT IS SAFE TO SAY, most contemporary Americans were confident and trusting in their government leadership. While there were always those who didn't agree with all the positions and policies of the sitting president, the majority believed that he was acting in the best interests of the nation. Law-abiding citizens could draw comfort from the belief that their elected leaders were making decisions, writing legislation, and forming policies that served the needs of the population. Even if they didn't understand the hows and whys of governmental procedure, they assumed that their leaders would handle affairs of state with due honor and efficiency.

That all changed during the Vietnam War. While there is little doubt that the main damage caused by the conflict was the massive loss of human life, the relationship between the American people and their government also suffered extensive damage.

Origins of the War

In the early part of the twentieth century the Asian nation now known as Vietnam was governed by France. That changed in 1940, when Vietnam was invaded by Japanese troops during World War II. The Vietnamese people hadn't particularly liked being governed by France, and Japanese rule didn't seem much better. So Vietnamese soldiers attacked the Japanese at every opportunity. They were aided by the U.S. military—the United States wanted not just to prevent Japan from taking over Vietnam but to keep Japan and its allies in Nazi Germany and Fascist Italy from taking over the world.

When Japan surrendered at the end of World War II (in 1945), the United States expected Vietnam to return to its previous colonial relationship with France. But many of the Vietnamese people, led by a man known as Ho Chi Minh, had a different idea. Ho saw an opportunity to turn Vietnam into an independent country. He felt his destiny was to lead the Vietnamese people to a better future. He also believed in the political philosophy of communism—the idea that people should put the interests of their society before personal concerns. The new communist government would control all the businesses, public utilities, and so on, and everyone would essentially be a government employee. For example, if the government felt more engineers were needed, some people would be told to become engineers—even if they aspired to do something else.

The United States, founded on the belief in the right to pursue individual freedom (the direct opposite of communism), didn't want Vietnam to fall under the control of Ho. If that happened, many in the U.S. government feared communism would quickly spread to other Asian nations.

France, of course, wanted to regain control of Vietnam. So with limited but necessary help from the United States, the French fought Ho Chi Minh's forces throughout the mid-1940s and into the 1950s. But Ho's armies proved tougher than expected, and France never regained control. Instead, a temporary agreement was reached in 1954 that split Vietnam into two parts—North Vietnam, governed by Ho Chi Minh and his communist followers, and South Vietnam, eventually governed by Ngo Dinh Diem, who had been placed in power by the United States to fight off the further spread of communism. At the time, President Eisenhower told Diem, "You have brought to your great task of organizing your country the greatest of courage, the greatest of statesmanship." The American government was, obviously, feeling optimistic about Diem's success.

The problem was, Diem was unpopular with almost all the Vietnamese people, and with good reason: he used the military to steal land from farmers, he executed political opponents (often without trial), and he gave wealthy people preferential treatment. It wasn't long before most of the South Vietnamese people wanted Diem out of office. America wanted him to stay, however, because he was willing to fight the communist movement in the north. Unsurprisingly, then, a group known as the National Liberation Front (NLF) formed in South Vietnam in support of Ho Chi Minh. Opposed by the NLF, Ho's forces, and thousands of angry South Vietnamese civilians, Diem began to lose control. He was murdered on November 2, 1963, plunging South Vietnam into even greater instability.

America's Increased Involvement

By 1964 the American government was more concerned than ever about the spread of communism from North Vietnam. With the South Vietnamese government in disarray, U.S. president Lyndon Johnson thought about increasing his country's involvement in the fighting. First, however, he

Ho Chi Minh's Early Travels

Ho Chi Minh left Vietnam in 1911 to travel and learn about Western culture and politics. He began his journey by working in a ship's kitchen while en route to France, where he worked at menial jobs during the day and visited libraries at night. He also lived and studied in America for a few years, then moved on to England. He eventually returned to France, then left again for brief stays in the Soviet Union, China, Germany, Switzerland, Italy, and Thailand. He returned to Vietnam in 1941, wiser and more educated, and began his crusade to lead the Vietnamese people to independence from colonial rule.

The Gulf of Tonkin Incident — Fact or Fiction?

The two attacks on American warships that eventually gave President Johnson leverage to greatly expand American involvement in the Vietnamese conflict comprised what is known as the Gulf of Tonkin Incident. The U.S. government told the people that the American vessel *Maddox* was fired upon by three Vietnamese patrol boats on August 2. Two days later, both the *Maddox* and a second ship, the *Turner Joy*, were targets of a second attack. However, there is now strong evidence that the *Maddox* may have fired *first* on August 2, and that the second attack may not have occurred at all.

It has also been suggested that the U.S. ships were on a spy mission and violating international waters in the first place. Nevertheless, the Gulf of Tonkin incident was the basis upon which America entered one of the most nightmarish periods in its history.

needed a reason for sending troops that the American people would understand and support.

On August 2 an American warship was fired upon by a smaller North Vietnamese vessel. In response President Johnson sent more American warships into the region. Then, on August 4 a second attack reportedly occurred. It is now believed, however, there was no shooting on August 4. In any event, Johnson first told America, "We still seek no wider war," then decided to launch a direct assault on North Vietnamese forces in response.

The war carried on for the next four years, brutal and bloody, with no clear sign of who was winning or losing.

Young American soldiers, many as young as eighteen, fought in the Vietnam War.

Vietnamese people on both sides were being killed by the millions, while towns and villages burned to the ground. Air Force General Curtis LeMay wrote in 1965, "My solution to the problem would be to tell [the North Vietnamese] frankly that they've got to draw in their horns and stop their aggression, or we're going to bomb them back into the Stone Age." President Johnson continued pouring money into the conflict while sending thousands of young men to their deaths in the Vietnamese jungles.

Outcry at Home

Some Americans became frustrated and angry about the Vietnam War. A politically charged group known as the New Left had much to say about it long before the rest of the nation did. The New Left was made up mostly of young people, many of them students, who held views that were often well to the left of the beliefs of more moderate liberals. Many saw the young group members as extreme and uncompromising, and soon the label "radical" was attached to the New Left and its supporters. Nevertheless, the New Left found a cause in the Vietnam War that brought their voices to national attention. Their leaders wondered, for example, if President Johnson really was interested in protecting freedom and liberty in Vietnam, since previous administrations had supported Diem, who was essentially a dictator who was hardly interested in the personal freedoms of his people. Also, what did Vietnam's freedom have to do with America's? Did a communist-ruled Vietnam really pose an imminent threat? The left in general was also concerned that the American government's power was growing too great and that officials were practicing a subtle form of colonial rule—acting as if they could conquer and reshape whatever regions met with their disapproval, and who could stop them? Finally, the New Left was justifiably angry because the average age of the American soldiers in Vietnam was nineteen.

Whether the New Left was overly radical or not, people were listening to its spokespeople. Starting in 1965 many Americans—even moderate liberals—began to formally and actively protest the war, beginning with several teach-ins, where faculty and students in various colleges got together to discuss the war's impact. Young people were particularly sensitive to this topic because they were the ones being drafted to do the actual fighting. One protest group known as the Mobe (National Mobilization Committee to End the War in Vietnam) organized a march with the following statement:

> We march to dramatize the world wide hope
> that the United States remove its troops
> from Vietnam so that the Vietnamese can
> determine their own future in their own
> way. We call for the enlistment of men,
> money, and resources now being used to
> maintain the military machine in a fight
> against the real enemies of man—hunger,
> hopelessness, ignorance, hate, discrimination
> and inequality. As the war cruelly destroys in
> Vietnam, so it denies hope to millions in the
> United States.

There were more public activities, such as marches and rallies—and they were shown on television, allowing people across the nation to watch and learn. And as President Johnson sent more troops to Vietnam, more American citizens began taking part in the protests. Millions demanded to know

In November 1969, 20 to 30 million Vietnam War protestors took to the streets of Washington, D.C., to march in the Peace Moratorium.

why the war was dragging on so long, when it would end, and whether the American government had been fully truthful about the reasons for getting involved in the first place.

In spite of all this a large segment of Americans stood by the war and its intentions, and thus opposed the antiwar movement. Those who held these more conservative beliefs criticized protesters, calling them unpatriotic and unaware of the magnitude of what was at stake. They said the protesters didn't understand the dangers of appeasing invaders such as Ho Chi Minh. When the Nazi leader Adolf Hitler was handed Czechoslovakia in 1938 under the assumption that he would then refrain from waging war elsewhere in Europe, did it work out that way? Of course not. These young protesters, conservatives said, didn't take the lessons of history into consideration. If they did, they would understand the value of the conflict in Vietnam.

In 1967 Johnson made several attempts to calm the public. In speeches he implied that an end was in sight and that he was confident of a positive outcome. He told the American people that he could see the "light at the end of the tunnel." Then in January 1968 came an attack known as the Tet Offensive—a massive and unexpected assault on American and South Vietnamese troops. The enormous cost in human, military, and economic terms motivated more people in America than ever before to become involved in the antiwar movement. It seemed that there was no clear way to victory and that the United States had no viable exit strategy. It also made Americans more suspicious and distrustful of President Johnson's administration. It was, without question, the turning point for many American citizens.

The Vietnam War had become a national nightmare.

Three

Further Unrest

THOSE WHO WANTED TO WIPE OUT RACISM and/or halt the fighting in Vietnam weren't the only ones rallying for change in the 1960s. The "counterculture movement" consisted of several other groups as well, all of whom contributed to the spirit of the era and thus deserve mention.

The Women's Movement

There was a time when women had a greatly reduced, limited, and in many ways humiliating role in American society. For example, until the Nineteenth Amendment to the U.S. Constitution was added in 1920, women didn't even have the right to vote in political elections. Prior to the social upheaval of the 1960s, a woman's "place" in society was defined largely as someone who should stay at home, have and raise children, and depend on a husband for all financial support. Famed feminist Betty Friedan wrote in 1963:

> The problem lay buried, unspoken, for many years in the minds of American women. It was a strange stirring, a sense of dissatisfaction, a yearning that women suffered in the middle of the twentieth

century in the United States. Each suburban
wife struggled with it alone. As she made
the beds, shopped for groceries, matched
slipcover material, ate peanut butter
sandwiches with her children, chauffeured
Cub Scouts and Brownies, lay beside her
husband at night—she was afraid to ask even
of herself the silent question "Is this all?"

The few women who did work outside the home usually
only did so on a part-time basis, and their pay was incom-
parable to that of a man doing the same work. Also, women
rarely held positions of any great importance. In an office
environment, for example, they would take messages, write
letters, keep files in order, and so forth. But they did not
make key decisions in the running of a business and were
therefore not looked upon as leaders. This kept them in a
"secondary" layer of society, where their work was dispens-
able, and they posed no threat to men.

Spurred by the many other social movements of the late
1950s and early 1960s, however, an increasing number of
women began to react to these unjust practices. For the first
time in history they began speaking out as a group, demanding more respect and better treatment. Young women strove to
attend the finest colleges with the intent that they would join
the workforce—and leave their mark upon it—after gradua-
tion. Many favored the idea of "role reversal" between a man
and a woman, suggesting that they be the ones who earn the
money while their male partners stay at home and raise children. Some chose not to have any children at all. Some women
even took pride in remaining single, defying the age-old notion
that a woman was defined by her husband, that is, a woman

The Nineteenth Amendment and the Silent Sentinels

On January 10, 1917, a group of women gathered outside the White House to protest the fact that they had no voice in public elections—in short, women were not allowed to vote. The group, led by Alice Paul (feminist and cofounder of the National Women's Party), carried signs and marched around the streets. Some were eventually arrested and thrown in jail, where they were treated harshly and forced to endure horrid conditions. Neverthless, the Silent Sentinels continued their protest in front of the White House until June of 1919—*two and a half years later*—when both the Senate and the House of Representatives proposed the Nineteenth Amendment, giving American women the right to vote. It became law one year later.

National Organization for Women president Betty Friedan marches with fellow feminists on the fiftieth anniversary of the passing of the Nineteenth Amendment.

had to be married—and if she wasn't, there was something wrong with her.

The Civil Rights Act of 1964 provided some much-needed progress in this area, when the word "sex" was added to the section about discrimination that previously only protected people of color. After the act was passed, women could no longer be rejected for jobs on the basis of their gender. However, as with many other aspects of the Civil Rights Act, it was tough getting people to obey the new laws. The same problem applied to sexual harassment—the act of mistreating a woman based on a sexual premise. Unfortunately, it was and still is an all-too-common problem in the workplace. Women were regarded by some men as little more than objects of beauty. As a result, women often became the victim of distasteful comments and gestures, and some even had their job security threatened if they were unwilling to welcome a man's advances.

By the late 1960s women had gained some ground in their fight for equality, but they still had a long way to go.

The Environmental Movement

Concern for the health of the planet and its natural resources is not a new idea, but it has definitely taken on a larger role—and greater urgency—since the beginning of the Industrial Age. As humankind has acquired a better understanding of advanced technologies, we have also developed an unfortunate tendency to damage the natural environment that we depend upon for our survival.

In America awareness of this problem existed as far back as the 1700s. But its true rise to prominence probably began in the 1800s, both with the publication of Henry David Thoreau's groundbreaking book *Walden*, in 1854, and the tireless work of John Muir, the founder of the Sierra Club who is considered the father of modern environmentalism. *Walden* chronicled Thoreau's stay in an isolated cabin on Walden Pond, in Massachusetts, where he attempted to gain a better understanding of nature by "becoming a part of it." Muir, similarly, spent many years wandering through the undeveloped areas of the United States, wrote many essays and books on the subject, and worked with several politicians (including President Theodore Roosevelt) to raise public awareness of and gain legal protection for certain areas.

The U.S. population exploded after World War II (this eventually became known as the Baby Boom era), and with that came the demand for more housing, more cars, more roads, more luxury products . . . more everything. Factories and laborers were working around the clock to meet this demand—and, in turn, the environment suffered. Forests were bulldozed to clear space for office buildings and housing developments. Rivers and lakes were polluted as manufacturers dumped their toxic waste in them. The problem was, few people at the time realized the damage being done.

One who did, however, was a biologist named Rachel Carson. Carson wrote a book published in 1962 called *Silent Spring*. Carson, who was already an experienced author and scientist, presented solid evidence that certain chemical products were causing irreparable harm to many forms of wildlife (particularly birds), and that the government wasn't doing much to curtail the activities of the companies responsible. In one powerful passage she wrote:

> During the past quarter century this power has not only increased to one of disturbing magnitude but it has changed in character.

The Baby Boom in the United States

Fewer couples were having children before World War II because America, just like many other nations, was still reeling from the effects of the Great Depression. After the war, however, the American economy not only recovered, it experienced a period of unprecedented growth. America was helping Europe and Asia rebuild their shattered infrastructures in the wake of the conflict, and that meant more jobs, more opportunities, and more money for the American people. It also meant more children—in times of economic prosperity, it is not uncommon for couples, feeling secure about their financial situation, to decide the time is right to begin or expand their families. (In 1950 alone almost 3.5 million babies were born.) Today, adults born between the years 1946 and 1964 are known as Baby Boomers.

> The most alarming of all man's assaults upon
> the environment is the contamination of air,
> earth, rivers, and sea with dangerous and
> even lethal materials. This pollution is for
> the most part irrecoverable; the chain of evil
> it initiates not only in the world that must
> support life but in living tissues is for the
> most part irreversible.

The book sold millions of copies and inspired conservation awareness across the nation. More alarming information surfaced about plant and animal species that had been driven to extinction by human carelessness and insensitivity, and by the mid-1960s, dozens of environmental groups had formed, joining ranks with the other social movements of the decade.

The Gay Rights Movement

Inspired by other social movements of the 1950s and 1960s, many people of homosexual orientation found the courage to take action against their own discriminatory burdens. Homosexuality—the physical and emotional attraction to someone of the same rather than the opposite gender—was regarded in America as everything from an illness to a crime. Many who were "diagnosed" as homosexual in their youth were subjected to treatments varying in severity from psychological examination to electroshock therapy. Homosexual practices were forbidden by law in almost every state. In the mid 1950s President Dwight D. Eisenhower issued an executive order forbidding gays (a synonym for "homosexuals") from entering the military or being employed in any government-run agencies or departments. And those who decided to join the military

Standing up and speaking out, homosexuals rally for their rights in New York in 1970.

anyway, even in the interest of serving his or her country, lived in perpetual fear of being "found out" and punished. The exact wording of the order was somewhat gray in nature but clear in its intent—people who could be investigated and possibly removed from service included those who practiced "Any criminal, infamous, dishonest, immoral, or notoriously disgraceful conduct, habitual use of intoxicants to excess, drug addiction, [or] sexual perversion."

Several law-enforcement agencies also kept a watch on high-profile homosexuals, and once the government put its official seal of approval on this type of discrimination, businesses and organizations quickly followed. Homosexuals who had strong professional qualifications, for example, found it all but impossible to find jobs. Gays were also targets of mistreatment outside the workplace, often subject to public abuse ranging from name-calling to brutal physical attacks. And although such attacks were against the law, those who carried out these horrendous acts were rarely prosecuted.

But in the 1960s, while so many other groups were standing up for themselves, homosexuals decided the time was right to do the same. At first their efforts were subtle, almost invisible. New gay bars, for example, opened in various towns and cities, where homosexuals could gather, form friendships, and generally feel safe from society's scrutiny. Then action groups began to organize, and they held marches and other protests in order to increase public awareness of their plight. Newspapers and magazines focusing on gay rights issues began appearing, and soon a formal movement, demanding fair and equal treatment, was under way.

PART II: EXPLOSION

A RIOT, BY DEFINITION, is a public and chaotic act of civil disorder carried out by a group of people in the spirit of protest. It usually involves violence and destruction and often results in extensive property damage, personal injury, and on occasion, death. Rioting is against the law and almost always requires a response by law enforcement.

The core cause of rioting has never changed—*anger*. But the precipitating factors that bring about the anger vary from political opposition and government oppression to poor living conditions, unfair employment practices, and so on. In certain cases protests that began peacefully have flared into full-scale riots due to the presence of individuals determined to escalate the tension of a given situation. Such people are often called agitators and are extremely dangerous. Similarly, riots have sometimes arisen because of false information—in the form of rumors, suppositions, or outright lies—and led to the unnecessary ruination of entire communities. In these situations the participants didn't realize their anger was baseless until after the damage was done.

Because of all these variables, viewpoints on the justification of rioting are numerous. To radical leftists rioting is a form of expression, a form of rebellion, and a form of equalization. Radicals feel that riots are an indispensible last resort that, when utilized, underscore the fact that all other options have been exhausted—and thus, they are justified. For more moderate liberal types, riots are frowned upon due to their violent nature—but they are still tolerated to some degree. More often than not the people who take part in riots share similar political views with moderate liberals, just make them heard in a more extreme fashion. A rough comparison would be the relationship between naughty children and forgiving parents—the parents (the moderate liberals) accept a certain amount of bad behavior from the children (the radical leftists) until the children go too far, in which case the parents finally step in and act. Finally, there are the conservatives, who generally regard rioters as outlaws. Conservatives are generally against "bucking comformity" and "rocking the boat," and thus they have little patience for those who practice civil disobedience. In their minds breaking the law is breaking the law, and it is rare to find a conservative with a sympathetic view toward those who willfully wreak havoc on people and their communities.

Even the vocabulary is hotly contested—should these events really be called riots, or something else? What about "outbursts" or "civil explosions" or "incidents of social unrest?" "Civil disorder" is a commonly used phrase, favored by conservatives because it focuses on the lawlessness of the act. But those on the radical left find it insulting because it suggests disobedience. Other popular terms include "uprising," "revolution," "rebellion," and "insurrection." All do an adequate job of describing the actions involved in a riot, but is one more correct than the others?

Emotions run high during periods of civil unrest. These events have been given names such as "civil explosions" and "civil disorder."

Law-enforcement agencies have two basic approaches to quelling a riot—passively and aggressively. With the passive approach, they attempt to contain and, in a sense, control the rioters until their rage is exhausted. For example, police surround a riot zone to keep the riot from spreading, but they do not engage the rioters face-to-face unless absolutely necessary. One of the advantages to this approach is that fewer people are usually harmed in the long run. An aggressive strategy, on the other hand, involves officers essentially becoming involved in the riot itself, putting themselves in harm's way as they try to squelch all violent activity. Tools at their disposal include nightsticks, trained dogs, various sprays and gases and, as a last resort, hardcore weaponry such as handguns and rifles.

Rioting has occurred throughout the world for many centuries, but in America in the 1960s it became something of a fad. As we have already learned, there was a strong sentiment of rebellion in many parts of American society after World War II, and the idea of mobilizing that rebellion—not just thinking about it or talking about it but *acting* upon it—inspired demonstrative displays of all kinds. For the many thousands who had suffered one massive disappointment after another—most of whom were of a racial minority and therefore largely neglected by the larger society—rioting became the instrument of choice. It was not civilized, it was not subtle, and it was nowhere in the vicinity of legal. But most who chose it did so because they felt better courses of action were no longer available to them.

Let's examine some of the most important riots of the 1960s. These should help you better understand the basic pattern and profile of the rioting mentality.

Four

Some
Early Riots
of the 1960s

THE FIRST MAJOR RACE RIOT OF THE 1960S occurred in the
two New York neighborhoods of Harlem and Bedford-
Stuyvesant, in July 1964. Before World War II these
had been predominantly white areas. After the war,
however, large numbers of whites bought homes in the
developing suburbs. "Between the end of World War II
and the early 1960s," writes sociology professor Janet
Abu-Lughod, "significant redistributions of New York's
racial and ethnic groups occurred. . . . Many young
newly formed families of working-class whites did not
return to the neighborhoods in which they grew up." This
massive exodus, or "white flight," left blacks and other
minorities with almost no employment opportunities,
living in decaying neighborhoods served by indifferent
local governments. Furthermore, although Harlem and
Bedford-Stuyvesant were occupied mostly by blacks, the
police forces assigned to the neighborhoods were over-
whelmingly white. All these factors, combined with the
civil rights movement that was growing in the southern
states, created tremendous tension in the area.

The incident that sparked the 1964 riots was the fatal shooting of a fifteen-year-old black youth by a white police officer on July 16. The teenager, James Powell, had been loitering in front of an apartment building, and the superintendent tried to chase him away. Powell refused to leave, however, and an off-duty police officer, Thomas Gilligan, rushed to the scene. After a brief confrontation, the details of which have never been clear, Gilligan, who was in civilian clothes, drew his gun and fired three shots, the second of which killed Powell.

The black communities in both neighborhoods responded swiftly and angrily. The people felt that Gilligan had used unnecessary force and demanded that he be relieved of duty and charged with homicide. Community leaders, however, refused to do anything until an official investigation was concluded—and blacks soon took to the streets in protest. At first the demonstrations were peaceful enough but, pressured by the continuing presence of the mostly white police force and the refusal by local government to act, they soon turned ugly. One reporter for *The New Yorker* who was on the scene remembers, "[I] was threatened by a group of Negroes but was given a chance to scurry to safety by a Negro youth who distracted the mob."

Marches descended into all-out brawls, bottles and bricks rained down from rooftops, stores were looted, and fires burned everywhere. In an effort to keep the situation from growing worse, police resisted the urge to use enough force to bring a halt to the rioting. But soon the violence escalated on both sides. The rioting continued almost without pause until July 23—a full week after the Powell shooting. In the

Sparked by the shooting of a fifteen-year-old black teenager, a riot ensued in 1964 in Harlem that included looting, arson, and violence.

end several additional people lay dead, hundreds more were injured, over four hundred arrests were made, and millions of dollars in damage had been done.

Perhaps worst of all, a pattern had been set—the Harlem–Bedford-Stuyvesant riots would serve as a blueprint for other such uprisings in the years ahead.

The Harlem Fruit Riot of 1964

Before the brutal Harlem–Bedford-Stuyvesant riot of 1964, there had been an earlier conflict. The Harlem Fruit Riot, which occurred in April 1964, was relatively smaller in scope but likely contributed to the rising tension between area residents and the local police force. There are conflicting accounts about the exact details of the incident, but it seems that a group of black children, walking home from school, tried to steal a few apples and oranges from a fruit and vegetable stand. As a result, the stand overturned, spilling produce everywhere. When four police officers tried to catch the children and beat them with nightsticks, some neighborhood teenagers and a few adults who tried to intervene on the children's behalf were also beaten as more police arrived on the scene to act as backups. In the end many people were injured; one black man lost his right eye.

Philadelphia, Pennsylvania (1964)

The rioting that occurred in northern Philadelphia in August 1964 was, in many ways, eerily similar to the Harlem–Bedford-Stuyvesant riots from the previous month. First, there was the community itself—for years a mixture of races, at that point a predominantly black neighborhood. There were grim economic issues: many families barely surviving, jobs in short supply, and little hope of a better future. And perhaps worst of all, there was growing resentment between the citizens and the law-enforcement agencies—as in New York the police were largely white, while the population was largely black. To make matters worse, local newspapers had published numerous reports of police brutality in recent months. In most cases the officers were either acquitted of any charges or not charged at all. With all these elements mixed together, the situation was ripe for violence.

That violence erupted on August 28, 1964. In the evening a woman named Odessa Bradford was driving down Columbia Avenue when her car stalled. Two police officers—one white, the other black—approached and told her to move the car off the road. Bradford tried to oblige but was unsuccessful—the car wouldn't budge, and she had no idea how to get it started. The officers were unsympathetic, and a heated argument followed. When the policemen tried to forcibly remove the driver from the vehicle, she began fighting back. A passerby noticed the struggle and rushed to Bradford's assistance. In the end the police arrested both of them.

Under normal circumstances the incident would have ended there. Instead, an angry crowd formed, and a rumor spread that two white policemen had beaten a pregnant black woman to death. Gerald Early, a resident of the area at the

Looting takes place in the open as mobs riot in Philadelphia in 1964.

time, remembers, "Rumor spread along Columbia Avenue and its environs that a pregnant black woman had been beaten to death by a white cop. This rumor was started by Raymond Hall, 25, a neighborhood agitator affiliated with no political organization." The untrue rumor was believed, causing the crowd to turn vengeful, and soon people began rioting. Hundreds rushed to the scene, and the original crowd split into several mobs. They roamed the area all night and throughout the next two days, smashing store windows, stealing goods, and setting buildings ablaze.

At first the police tried to restore order, but they quickly realized they were outnumbered and helpless. Police Commissioner Howard Leary ordered his officers to leave the area and wait for the riot to run its course rather than risk their lives. Also, several black leaders pleaded with the rioters to calm down. Later, part of Columbia Avenue was renamed in honor of one of these spokesmen, the notable lawyer and civil rights activist Cecil B. Moore.

In the end the toll was enormous—over three hundred people injured, more than twice that many arrested, and millions of dollars' worth of damage to city and private properties. Gerald Early also noted, "A few years ago, a black lawyer told me that when, as a teenager going to school, she walked along Columbia Avenue a few days after the riot, the smashed plate glass was nearly ankle-deep. It crunched under her feet like an icy snow." Many business owners simply left town without cleaning up what remained of their shops. And no new businesses replaced them, which drove the area into even deeper economic ruin. To this day Columbia Avenue remains one of the poorest sections of Philadelphia.

Los Angeles (Watts), California (1965)

Commonly known as the Watts riots but actually taking place throughout several sections of Los Angeles were some of the bloodiest and most costly uprisings of the decade. As with those in New York and Pennsylvania, they grew out of a relatively minor incident—but at a time when long-brewing anger had just about reached the boiling point.

In the early twentieth century Los Angeles was home to people of many ethnic backgrounds—Mexicans, Asians, blacks, whites, and others. During World War II, however, the black portion of the population, drawn to the area by the ready availability of jobs in support of the war effort, increased dramatically. New houses and apartments were being built, new lines of transportation in and out of the area were being established, and so on. The city was experiencing a period of growth and prosperity.

When the war ended, however, most of the factories and other businesses either closed or relocated. Wealthier residents followed them out of the area, setting their sights on better housing opportunities and higher-paying jobs. The community began to fade until all that remained were the underprivileged poor, most of whom were black. With little hope or opportunity, their resentment, augmented by concern over police mistreatment, began to fester. Many turned to crime, and alcohol and drug use increased. By the mid-1960s some Los Angeles neighborhoods were on the verge of explosion.

As with the Philadelphia riots of 1964, the match that lit the fuse was a routine traffic stop. On the evening of August 11 a black citizen told a white officer of the California Highway Patrol that he had seen someone driving erratically. The patrolman tracked down the car, pulled it over, and gave the driver, a young black man, a sobriety test. The test determined that the driver was, in fact, drunk. The officer then decided to arrest the driver and have his car towed away. The driver, along with his brother (who was in the passenger seat), argued with the officer, but to no avail. Realizing that he would not be able to talk his way out of the arrest, the driver became angry. Meanwhile, a crowd of neighbors began to form. Then the mother of the two men arrived on the scene. After arguing both with her sons and with the police, she attacked one of the officers. By this time several other officers had come to act as backup. The mother was also arrested, and while she and her sons were being taken from the scene, a young woman in the crowd spat at the police. She was arrested as well. As the police left with the four arrestees, their vehicles were attacked by several members of the crowd, who threw stones and bottles.

The incident should have ended right there. Instead, the crowd—now numbering in the hundreds—broke into smaller groups as false rumors started by an agitator spread throughout the area. One was that the girl who had spat on the police and was arrested was pregnant. Another was that the officers had treated her and the other suspects with unnecessary force and cruelty. Fueled by this misinformation, the mobs began roaming, and the rioting began. More vehicles were damaged; people who had had nothing to do with the original incident were beaten at random. Police were threatened and harassed, and more officers were called in for added protection. One eyewitness was Betty Pleasant, at the time an editor for the *Los Angeles Sentinel*. She remembers:

> We got a couple of calls from people stating
> that something is happening at Imperial
> Highway and Central Avenue and we ought
> to check it out. "What?" we asked. "I dunno.
> Something," they answered. We shrugged
> our shoulders and ignored it. Then more calls
> came in. They were more frantic and explicit.
> They said: "Pigs are beating Negroes and
> Negroes are fighting back!" Mercy!!!

Earlier Tension in the Watts Area

The situation in Watts, in which an agitator spread the rumor that police were mistreating a pregnant woman, may have been inspired by an earlier incident in the area that did, in fact, involve white police officers and a pregnant black woman. On May 7 a pair of white policemen on patrol had pulled over a black man for speeding. The man had been rushing to the hospital, with his pregnant wife in the passenger seat. One of the officers aimed his pistol at the driver, and seconds later the weapon discharged, killing the man instantly. Whether the shot was intentional or accidental became a point of speculation. The officer, who was cleared of all charges, argued that the car had unexpectedly moved forward, causing the gun to fire inadvertently. But black residents in the area were suspicious, and their anger likely contributed to the tension that led to the Watts outbreak.

By the following morning the situation had generally calmed down—but community leaders were fearful of more violence that night. A meeting was held early in the afternoon, attended by people of all races. The hope was that the tension could be dialed down and resolved in a rational, sensible manner. This wasn't what happened, however. Instead, several members of the black community, tired of airing their grievances to the white leadership and getting few or no results, encouraged like-minded citizens to continue rioting. By early evening word had spread, and the riots began anew. More police were called to the area, and the California National Guard was told to be ready. The riot zone was surrounded by officers in an attempt to contain the violence. It raged throughout the night as fires were lit, windows were smashed, and businesses were looted.

The third day, a Friday, began calmly enough. By late morning, however, the rioting had restarted and was more vicious then ever. Fires were set on block after block, expanding the riot zone and destroying businesses that had been in the area for years. Firefighters who came in to quell the blazes were attacked. Police who tried to fight off the rioters to let the firefighters do their jobs were also attacked. Screams and cries filled the air, mingling with the crackle of tall flames, the sound of windows being smashed, and the occasional burst of gunfire. Thousands of angry residents clashed with police and National Guardsmen, and blood literally ran in the streets. Most horribly, as day turned to night, the death toll began to mount.

By Saturday morning the worst was over. There would be further incidents over the next three days, but nothing like Friday. A curfew was imposed, and fire departments

Fires burn throughout the Watts area in Los Angeles, the center of the 1965 race riots.

finally were able to put out most of the serious blazes. Aid stations were set up to provide food, water, and temporary housing. But this was only the start of the healing because Watts lay in ruins. Like a scene from a movie about nuclear war, there was nothing left. In the end over thirty people were killed and more than a thousand injured. Nearly four thousand arrests were made, and more than $40 million worth of damage was done to homes and businesses.

It is worth noting that some suggested the riots might have been planned by radical, conspiratorial figures waiting in the shadows for the right opportunity. This idea was investigated and eventually dismissed in a report given to the California governor in December 1965:

> After a thorough examination, the Commission has concluded that there is no reliable evidence of outside leadership or pre-established plans for the rioting. The testimony of law enforcement agencies and their respective intelligence officers supports this conclusion. The Attorney General, the District Attorney, and the Los Angeles police have all reached the conclusion that there is no evidence of a pre-plan or a pre-established central direction of the rioting activities. This finding was submitted to the Grand Jury by the District Attorney.

The "Long, Hot Summer" (1967)

America suffered more than a hundred incidents of civil unrest during 1967, many of which occurred during the warmer months—a period later called the "long, hot summer."

In Tampa, Florida, for example, police responded to a call on June 11 that a camera store was being robbed. Two officers arrived to find three black male teenagers fleeing the scene. They shouted for the teens to stop but were ignored. They repeated the order twice more but were again ignored. One of the officers then took out his pistol and fired a shot, which struck and killed one of the teens. Even though the officer had followed departmental procedure, rioting by an enraged black community erupted throughout the area. Soon, buildings were ablaze, stores were being looted, people were being openly beaten, and bullets were flying. The National Guard was summoned, but two days of intense rioting resulted in numerous injuries and arrests, plus millions of dollars in damage.

In Newark, New Jersey, a black cab driver was arrested on July 12. During the arrest the man sustained multiple injuries, and rumors quickly spread in the economically depressed area that he had been brutalized by police. Rocks and Molotov cocktails were hurled at officers at the Fourteenth Precinct station, followed the next day by widespread looting, and the day after that by violence against people. The National Guard was called in, but order was not restored for six days. In the end twenty-three people lay dead. And in Plainfield, just 18 miles away, a similar riot had erupted two days after the one in Newark began. Again, buildings were burned, there was wholesale looting, and innocent bystanders, as well as responding police and firefighters, were attacked. Unique to this incident, however, was the robbery of a company that manufactured semiautomatic carbines. Alarmed because such heavy arms were now in the possession of rioters, state police and National Guardsmen conducted door-to-door searches for the stolen weaponry.

By far the bloodiest riot of the 1967 summer occurred in Detroit, Michigan. Detroit was unlike other "riot cities" of the 1960s in that many blacks there earned decent salaries and lived in nice homes. The automotive industry was booming, providing thousands of jobs and keeping the area afloat economically. Detroit blacks did not, however, have a proportionate amount of political power, and the police force was mostly white. Furthermore, relations between the police and the numerous black citizens were frosty, owing to past incidents of police brutality. So there was some tension despite the more favorable economic conditions.

On the morning of July 23, a Sunday, police raided several private drinking establishments. The one on Twelfth Street was loaded with customers, all of whom were arrested. Before the drinkers could be removed, the arrestees had formed a mob. Rumors quickly spread that the officers were mistreating the arrestees, and violence broke out late in the morning. Rocks and bottles flew through the air, while storefront windows were smashed and buildings were set on fire. Looting occurred everywhere, with some people joining in for just this reason. "I heard a friend of mine say, 'Hey, they rioting up in Twelfth!'" recalled one black man. "I said what are they doing and he said looting. That's all it took to get me out of the house. . . . I said it was time for me to get some of these diamonds and watches and rings." The overwhelmed local authorities were soon joined by the Michigan State Police, then the National Guard. The heavy armed response only further enraged the black community, which in turn drove the need for even greater force—the U.S. Army. Paratroopers from the 82nd and 101st Airborne divisions, under the command of four-star general John Throckmorton, arrived on Tuesday. But still, another two days were needed to restore order.

The human cost of the Detroit riot was horrendous—43 dead and over 450 injured. More than 7,000 arrests were made; half of those detained had no prior criminal record. Over 2,500 buildings were looted or destroyed, and esti- mated property damage exceeded $40 million.

Michigan National Guardsmen were called to action during the 1967 race riots in Detroit.

An appalling body count had resulted from the "long, hot summer," along with rampant destruction in the Harlem–Bedford-Stuyvesant areas, Watts, and elsewhere around the nation. One might have thought that interracial tensions couldn't get any worse.

Then came April 1968.

Five

The Race Riots of 1968

MOST OF THE RACE RIOTS OF 1968 were driven by the same frustration that produced those of previous years, but with a new element. Through one criminal act of historic significance, the black community suddenly lost Martin Luther King Jr., the leader who had embodied their greatest hope for a better future. With King gone, many felt their chances for social equality had vanished. At a time when racial tension was at a fever pitch and rioting had become almost commonplace, the assassination of the man who had most eloquently called for nonviolent resistance ensured that more days of chaos, rage, and destruction lay ahead.

The Death of Dr. Martin Luther King Jr.

King was born in Atlanta, Georgia, in 1929. Like his father, he was a Baptist minister, and in 1954 he became pastor of the Dexter Avenue Baptist Church in Montgomery, Alabama. When Rosa Parks was arrested for having refused to give up her seat on a city bus in 1955, King, who had already gained local fame for his powerful speaking skills, was asked to lead a protest. He did such a magnificent job of raising awareness of the issue, and of other discriminatory practices against blacks in the area, that he was soon spending more time on civil rights activities than on his pastoral duties.

In this new role he took a decidedly nonviolent approach to diminishing racism, believing that aggressive, hostile action inspired more resistance toward the black cause, not less. In the years ahead this passive approach would transform King into a national figure, earn him a Nobel Peace Prize and, most important inspire sympathy for the black cause in places it had not existed before. He gave hundreds of speeches (some of which are still widely quoted), met with national leaders all the way up to President Lyndon Johnson, and helped create the Southern Christian Leadership Conference (SCLC), which augmented the efforts of the NAACP.

By 1968 King was focusing his efforts on economic issues: equal pay for blacks who performed the same work as whites, fairer hiring opportunities, improved job training, and so on. In late March he went to Memphis, Tennessee, in support of black sanitation workers who had been on strike to protest low wages and poor treatment. On April 3 he attended a rally at a local church, where he gave what would be the final speech of his life. The last eerily prophetic line was "Mine eyes have seen the glory of the coming of the Lord." The next day, a Thursday, he was struck down by a sniper's bullet just after 6 PM, while standing on the balcony of the Lorraine Motel. He was taken to nearby St. Joseph Hospital and was pronounced dead about an hour later.

The news came like a thunderbolt to the black community, reaching every person in every corner of the nation. Mississippian Thelma Eubanks remembers, "When we heard he was shot, everybody was devastated. We felt we had lost probably the only black man who had guts enough to be as brave as

James Earl Ray — Assassin or Not?

On June 8, 1968, escaped convict James Earl Ray was captured in an airport in London and placed under arrest for the murder of Martin Luther King Jr. He confessed to the killing the following March, although he withdrew the confession shortly thereafter. Neverthless, he was sentenced to ninety-nine years in prison. He always maintained that he was innocent and, in 1997, King's son Dexter met with him. Armed with information Ray had provided, Dexter King brought another man, Loyd Jowers, to trial. Jowers was eventually found guilty of taking part in Dr. King's murder, suggesting that there was, in fact, a conspiracy. Ray's participation in the crime, however, was never fully established, and he died in prison on April 23, 1998.

WANTED BY THE FBI

CIVIL RIGHTS - CONSPIRACY
INTERSTATE FLIGHT - ROBBERY
JAMES EARL RAY

FBI No. 405,942 G

Photographs taken 1960

Photograph taken 1968
(eyes drawn by artist)

Aliases: Eric Starvo Galt, W. C. Herron, Harvey Lowmyer, James McBride, James O'Conner, James Walton, James Walyon, John Willard, "Jim,"

DESCRIPTION

Age:	40, born March 10, 1928, at Quincy or Alton, Illinois (not supported by birth records)		
Height:	5' 10"	**Eyes:**	Blue
Weight:	163 to 174 pounds	**Complexion:**	Medium
Build:	Medium	**Race:**	White
Hair:	Brown, possibly cut short	**Nationality:**	American

he was. We felt a big loss. We felt there was not going to be another King, not like him." There was also rage—extreme rage. Arlam Carr, who was living in Birmingham, Alabama, at the time, said, "The day Martin Luther King was killed, I didn't see the flag at half staff at school. I walked into the auditorium and in anger threw my books down. Then I walked to the principal's office and I said, 'Why isn't the flag at half staff?' I felt they weren't giving Dr. King the respect that he was due."

Pushed beyond their limits, the black community reacted swiftly and angrily. More than a hundred riots erupted across the nation. Many were relatively minor—but others were so destructive that they forever altered the cities in which they occurred. Among the most emblematic were those in Baltimore; Washington, D.C.; and Chicago.

Baltimore, Maryland

Unlike many other riots that followed the King assassination, the one in Baltimore did not begin immediately. There were a few incidents on the night of April 4—several fires and a few acts of vandalism—but nothing of major consequence. For the most part the city was quiet. The following day, a Friday, was equally placid, but the Maryland National Guard was put on standby, owing to the uprisings elsewhere, particularly in nearby Washington, D.C.

The major unrest began the following Saturday. During the early afternoon a memorial service was held in King's honor, followed by an interdenominational religious service. As darkness fell, civility unraveled. Several stores were looted, fires were started, and police were attacked with rocks and bottles. Nearly six thousand National Guardsmen were called in, along with over a thousand local and state police officers, but the destruction continued. Two people (one black, one white) died in a fire, and another citizen was shot and killed. Maryland governor Spiro Agnew temporarily banned the sale of alcohol, gasoline, and weaponry and imposed a curfew between the hours of 11 PM and 6 AM This caused a drop in the rioting but did not bring it to a complete halt.

The following morning the violence began anew. Fire officials tried to control the blazes but were attacked and had to be protected by soldiers. Hospitals were overflowing with the injured, and emergency trauma centers were set up in other locations around the city, along with temporary shelters for the homeless. By early afternoon fires numbered in the hundreds, and the curfew was moved up to 4 PM. Hundreds of arrests were made, and military helicopters patrolled the city from above. Also, the overwhelmed Maryland National Guard was joined for the first time by federal troops.

Rioting continued unabated for the next two days as more soldiers were summoned and control of the area was given over to the military. Martial law was declared. At the same time rioters used more sophisticated tactics, communicating by means of walkie-talkies and planting crudely made bombs. Snipers in high windows and on rooftops shot at police, firefighters, and anyone else who tried to restore order. In some areas even other blacks were attacked. Larry Carson, a white reporter who was there, remembered:

> That Monday after the Rev. Martin Luther
> King Jr.'s murder was chaos in East
> Baltimore, where I struggled as a raw,
> 23-year-old police reporter for the *News*

American to gather information. Strangely,
none of the looters gave me a second glance,
and I was calm and unafraid. Young, white,
with short hair and wearing a sportcoat and
tie, I probably looked like a police officer. I
overheard several actual officers lamenting
that since the new emphasis on civil rights,
they had to arrest suspects instead of taking
them around a corner and beating them.

Some semblance of order was restored by Wednesday,
April 10, and the worst of it was over—but the city lay in
ruins. Six people were dead and over a thousand injured.
More than 5,500 arrests were made, and at least a thousand
homes and businesses destroyed—roughly the same as the
number of fires that had been set.

Washington, D.C.

The riots that erupted in America's capital following King's
assassination began almost instantly. Washington, being the
epicenter of the nation's political activity, also made an ideal
headquarters for the civil rights movement. The NAACP had
an office there, as did the SCLC. And the black population,
initially attracted by plentiful government jobs in the era
following the fall of legal segregation, was large. Many black
families lived in crushing poverty, but others had achieved
middle-class status. Regardless of where they stood on the
economic ladder, however, all blacks in the area were aware
of their race's repressed position in society and the tiring
campaign to change it.

The intersection of Fourteenth and U streets was considered by many to be the heart of D.C.'s black district, and it was there that the unrest began. As King's murder became known via television and radio, a vengeful crowd (made up mostly, but not entirely, of black youths) began to form. Then another well-known black figure arrived on the scene—Stokely Carmichael, former King associate and leader of another activist organization, the Student Nonviolent Coordinating Committee (SNCC). Leading the crowd through the neighborhood, Carmichael went from store to store, requesting that all business be halted for the day out of respect for King's passing. Most obliged, later saying that Carmichael and his followers were polite and respectful. But, almost inevitably, some shop owners and managers refused to close, and some blacks had little interest in channeling their grief and anger in a responsible manner.

By nightfall full-scale rioting was well under way. Rocks and bottles flew through the air, windows in homes and businesses were smashed, goods were being stolen by the armful, and fires blazed everywhere. Community leaders both black and white pleaded for calm, but to no avail. Carmichael spoke at a rally the next day, and his speech reflected the anger felt by blacks nationwide. The general feeling was that with King himself murdered in cold blood, the strategy of peaceful protest no longer had any value, and aggressive action was the only effective tactic remaining. By the end of the day the rioting had started up again. Fires leapt from windows and danced along rooftops, broken glass littered the streets, and hundreds of alarms blared in unison to create a macabre soundtrack to the chaos.

Reginald Kelley, a black man who lived in D.C. at the time, said, "It was like total chaos. People running and screaming

Stokely Carmichael and the Black Panther Party

Stokely Carmichael was one of the most aggressive and outspoken black activists of the 1960s, preferring the fiery rhetoric of people like Malcolm X to the gentler strategies of Martin Luther King Jr. In 1966 Carmichael went to Alabama and formed the Lowndes County Freedom Organization (LCFO). When it came time to choose a representative image, he decided on a black panther. The media then began referring to the LCFO as the "black panther party." Some months later two other activists—Huey P. Newton and Bobby Seale—formed an organization by the same name in California. It went on to become the famous Black Panthers, a group that had some influence for a few years but faded in the late 1970s, when mounting legal costs and a growing reputation for violence caused many to rethink their earlier support.

After the assassination of Martin Luther King Jr., riots broke out in Washington, D.C.

with these fiendish looks on their faces. It was mob rule." Kelley saw a white man make the mistake of driving into the middle of the rioting and stop. What happened next was unforgettable: "Guys in their 20s and 30s pulled him from his car, started beating him mercilessly. When I saw blood start flying, that sickened me. I was scared and went home." Yet high school teacher Larry Aaronson, who is white, remembers being rescued by some of his black students. Knowing that black mobs were attacking white people at random, the teens burst into his classroom and said, "Larry, where is your car parked? Give us the keys!" They then herded him into his car and drove him away from the center of the violence. "I sat in my driver's seat, overwhelmed by emotions," Aaronson later admitted. "I broke down and cried. I cried for my kids, for my school, for my city. I cried for my country, for our movement. I cried for Dr. King and his family."

More than 3,000 policeofficers were called into the area, but they had little hope of controlling mobs that exceeded 20,000. President Johnson had little choice but to mobilize over 13,000 members of the military. Marines surrounding the White House and the Capitol had shoot-to-kill orders, and the roving crowd did move within a few blocks of the presidential mansion at one point. And again, as with so many other riots, firefighters trying to quell the blazes were attacked until the military provided them protection.

Order was restored after four long and harrowing days and nights. In the end the death count had risen to twelve (most of whom perished in house fires), and a thousand more were injured. Arrests topped six thousand, and double that number of homes and businesses were destroyed. Worst of all, the effect of the D.C. riot was in direct opposition to King's vision for his people—the black sections of the city plunged into even greater despair and economic disadvantage, and it would be many decades before any type of rebirth occurred.

Chicago, Illinois

Conditions for blacks in Chicago leading up to the King riots of 1968 were much the same as in other major cities—the squalid living conditions of poverty almost everywhere, minimal opportunities, and massive discontent, sometimes appearing as overwhelming depression, sometimes as anger. Throughout 1967, when many riots occurred elsewhere around the country, Chicago was relatively serene. Some attribute this to the policies of Mayor Richard J. Daley, a white Democrat who had, at different times, shown both compassion toward blacks and a willingness to crack down hard on anyone who violated the law.

The city was surprisingly quiet the night of King's assassination. The following day, however, law and order quickly diminished. There was a peaceful memorial service held in Dr. King's honor. But crowds gathered in outlying areas of the city and, driven by angry leaders who felt calm protest wouldn't be enough, began to cut a tornado-like path of destruction throughout Chicago's West Side—the poorest of the poor neighborhoods. Most of the rioters were of high school age, but a few were even younger. Windows and cars were smashed; garbage cans flew through the air along with rocks, sticks, and bottles; traffic lights and phone poles were pulled down; and buildings were set ablaze.

Every Chicago police officer—around five thousand in total—was called to duty. Told to use minimal force, they found themselves confronting rioters who attacked anyone in a uniform, including firefighters trying to quell the flames that leaped from hundreds of buildings and sanitation workers trying to clear the streets and sidewalks of bricks and glass. Within hours, Mayor Daley had requested that the governor send National Guardsmen. By midnight over 1,500 troops had arrived. The city quieted down after that, and it was hoped that the worst was over.

The next day, however, the rioting began again. This time it extended beyond the West Side and flared up in the South Side as well—more vicious than before. Police and guardsmen made hundreds of arrests, but it didn't seem to matter. If anything, their intervention only served to further enrage the rioters. Eventually President Johnson took the drastic step of ordering federal troops to the area. And Mayor Daley, like the mayors of other rioting cities, called for a curfew (7 PM for everyone under the age of twenty-one) and banned the sale of firearms, ammunition, alcohol, gasoline, and other items that would exacerbate the situation.

Following the second day's destruction Daley flew over the city by helicopter to assess the damage. What he saw both saddened and appalled him. Afterward, during a press conference in which he was still clearly agitated, he told reporters of a conversation he'd had with his police superintendent:

> I said to him very emphatically and very
> definitely that an order be issued by him
> immediately to shoot to kill any arsonist or
> anyone with a Molotov cocktail in his hand,
> because they're potential murderers, and to
> shoot to maim or cripple anyone looting.

Black leaders were outraged by these comments, and many feared the black community would launch a new wave of violence in retaliation. But Daley later backed down, restating that he wanted the police to use only as much force as necessary and no more. Nevertheless, he had created

The Chicago Race Riot of 1919

The city of Chicago was no stranger to rioting due to ethnic strife. In the summer of 1919 violence erupted following the death of a young black boy. Tensions had been brewing in the area for a while, as scores of black families emigrated following World War I, mostly to escape the social inequality in the southern states and to find available jobs in Chicago's growing industrial base. Unfortunately, many Chicago residents became resentful of the fast-growing black presence—suddenly there was greater competition for jobs and housing. Neighborhoods remained sharply segregated by race, with most blacks settling on Chicago's South Side.

On July 27 a group of young whites attacked a group of young blacks for having "invaded their space" on one of Chicago's lakeside beaches (even these were considered casually segregated). One of the black youths was struck on the head with a rock while in the water and drowned. Police summoned to the area, however, refused to arrest the white assailant. Fights broke out elsewhere nearby, and police began arresting blacks but not whites. Soon word spread across the Chicago "Black Belt," leading to full-scale riots that included public beatings, burglary, and arson. The outbreak lasted a full week and was finally quelled by more than five thousand National Guardsmen. In the end thirty-eight people were dead, over five hundred injured, and roughly a thousand left homeless.

more tension in the city—tension that would play a role in a second uprising before the end of the year.

The final tally of the Chicago riot was 11 dead, hundreds more injured, and over 2,000 people arrested (including about 350 minors). Scores of people were homeless, businesses were destroyed, and significant portions of the city's West Side, as well as parts of the South Side, had been reduced to rubble and would take decades to rebuild.

Differing Viewpoints

How does one consider the racially motivated riots of the 1960s? Who was right? Who was wrong? Conservatives saw the incidents as nothing more than criminal acts designed to undermine society's stability. They called out details supporting their claim that the majority of the rioters had little, if any, genuine passion for improving the treatment of black citizens. The looting, for example—how did this further the interests of blacks? If anything, conservatives asked, didn't it *reduce* their respectability? How did saying, "I am black and deserving of more respect" justify committing opportunistic theft? And the spreading of false rumors that sparked many of these outbreaks—how honorable was that? One agitator with the willingness to distribute a single lie could create mass hysteria within hours. Many conservatives saw only criminal behavior.

Radical leftists, however, took a very different stance. They felt the uprisings were fully justified in an ongoing battle against oppression by law enforcement and an elitist system run by privileged whites. Within this system, they argued, blacks were set on the lowest rung in society and were expected to stay there. In fact, to fully benefit this cruel system, blacks *needed* to stay there. It was all but impossible for blacks to climb any higher, as they had access only to the worst jobs, the poorest schools, the scantest opportunities. Violence, the New Left claimed, even if it carried legal penalties, was the only option available. In other words, if blacks wanted their collective voice to be heard, they could either mount violent protests or continue suffering under the heavy hand of the white power structure.

Moderate liberals were perhaps in the most difficult position of all. They had played a role in empowering many participants in the race riots. They had designed and implemented programs with the intention of helping hundreds of poor communities get on their feet. This goodhearted intention failed in so many places and in so many ways that liberals became disillusioned, confused, and divided. Thus by the end of the decade, radicals and conservatives agreed on one point—most of the government programs that were supposed to help blacks did anything but. It's no wonder that the liberally led Democratic Party was hopelessly dysfunctional by the end of the 1960s.

And thus the last great riot of the 1960s was all but inevitable.

Six

The 1968 Democratic National Convention Riots

EVERY FOUR YEARS each of the major political parties of the United States holds a gathering, called a convention, in which party leaders name their candidates for president and vice president in the coming general election. Each party nominates the individuals who appear to have the best chance of winning. It is also a time when leaders discuss the future policies and strategies of their party—which often leads to intense and heated debates. The conventions are always held in big cities and are widely covered by the media. While protests in the streets outside a party convention are not unusual, those of the 1968 Democratic National Convention in Chicago were, by far, the most violent in American history.

What made the convention riots fundamentally different from the race riots of 1968 was the basis of the rioters' anger—it wasn't about discrimination alone, it was about all the ills of American society. Most of all, people were infuriated by the government's handling of the Vietnam War, which had become a national nightmare. Many believed that the U.S. government had been manipulative and deceitful from the start, and that soldiers were being killed in a conflict that had no clear end in sight. Whereas about half the public had favored the war when it began, less than a quarter felt the same way by the summer of 1968. The protesters who showed up in Chicago that August demanded change—but the leader of the Democratic Party, President Lyndon Johnson, didn't seem willing to give it.

The People Involved

There is a certain "recipe" for civil unrest—and one of the ingredients is groups of passionate individuals with sharply different viewpoints. There was no shortage of such diverse thinkers at the 1968 convention.

A prominent viewpoint was represented by Mayor Daley and his law enforcement officials. After receiving criticism on numerous fronts for his handling of the race riots following the death of Martin Luther King Jr., Daley took a firm stance on security for the convention. Knowing that a strong feeling of protest was in the air and that tempers would probably reach a boiling point, some had suggested that the convention be moved elsewhere. But Daley insisted that law and order would be maintained—he had thousands of policeofficers on hand and National Guardsmen on standby. He also had undercover agents—both police and FBI—who had infiltrated the protestors' groups and were passing along information about their plans. Daley encouraged all of his law enforcement agents to keep things under control at any cost. Similarly, Roger Wilkins, the director of the Community Relations Service (part of the federal Department of Justice), wrote the following in a memo to the U.S. Attorney General:

> No matter what we do, the Mobilization
> and other organizations . . . will indeed
> produce in Chicago tens of thousands of
> people who are hostile to the Democratic

> Party, to President Johnson, and to Vice-
> President Hubert Humphrey . . . that large
> scale violence in Chicago at the time of the
> Convention would be a national disaster
> and a national disgrace; that such violence is
> possible and that our best chance of averting
> violence is to develop the closest possible
> working relationship between the Chicago
> authorities, the Democratic Party officials,
> federal officials and the Mobilization.

Clearly, federal and city government agencies were expecting trouble and planned to do everything in their power to prevent it.

The protesters, however, had no intention of staying within the boundaries of the law—their intent was to be seen and to have their opinions heard. They were mostly under the age of twenty-five, and the great majority was already involved in one cause or another—racial equality, the environment, women's rights, and so on. They were brought together by a common desire to use the occasion of the convention to change the Democratic Party's policy on the war. Some of the most famous names in the social movements of the 1960s were there, including Abbie Hoffman, cofounder of the Youth International Party (aka the Yippies); Jerry Rubin, another cofounder of the Yippies who also organized the Vietnam Day Committee; Rennie Davis, a prominent member of Students for a Democratic Society (SDS) and the National Mobilization Committee to End the War in Vietnam (the Mobilization); and Bobby Seale, a cofounder of the Black Panther Party. These activists were

Caught on Camera

During the 1968 convention, Democratic senator Abraham Ribicoff of Connecticut commented in a speech about "Gestapo tactics in the streets of Chicago." *Gestapo* was the name for the secret police acting on Adolf Hitler's behalf, known for their ruthless brutality in the Nazi era. Ribicoff, in turn, was referring to the harsh measures being used by the Chicago police force. Mayor Daley, embarrassed and enraged by the unexpected remark, fired back what appeared to be ethnic slurs at Ribicoff, who was Jewish. The mayor spoke away from the microphone so he wouldn't be heard by the crowd, but the outburst was caught on camera. Daley already had a reputation for using colorful and sometime ill-advised language, and this incident further damaged his reputation, which never fully recovered from the negative impact of his handling of the 1968 convention.

joined by thousands of others who shared their desire for change. Some had been to the antiwar marches elsewhere in the country, in which the crowd chanted to the president, "Hey, hey, LBJ, how many kids did you kill today?"

Even politicians within the Democratic Party were taking sides. President Johnson and his vice president, Hubert Humphrey, said they would continue the fighting in Vietnam until victory had been achieved—and most Democrats stood behind them. But others, such as Minnesota senator Eugene McCarthy, South Dakota senator George McGovern, and Attorney General Robert Kennedy (brother of assassinated president John F. Kennedy), favored a swift end to the war, feeling it had become too costly and was causing too much discord at home. All three men decided to seek the party's nomination for a presidential run, but Bobby Kennedy had been assassinated in June. That left McCarthy and McGovern, both of whom were very popular among antiwar Democrats. McGovern had made his position on the war and within the party very clear. Likewise, in his 1968 book *Eugene McCarthy on the Issues*, the Minnesotan had written, "What is new, and what is very much a product of the Administration's single-minded preoccupation with the war . . . is the feeling that these problems are not being solved *and are not about to be solved*. It is the disappearance of *hope* . . . that is the most unsettling fact about America." However, the prowar Democrats, who had the most power within the party, wanted Humphrey to be the next presidential nominee—and Humphrey, most assuredly, would keep the war going.

The final ingredient in the "recipe for civil unrest" was a group that is traditionally without an agenda—the media—newspaper and magazine writers, plus television reporters, most of whom were accompanied by photographers or cameramen. Since it was their job to capture the events and relay them back to the public, their role in the riots would be enormous. They stood in the center of the action and produced words and images that shocked and stunned the world. Even before the real rioting began, one reporter noted, "To reach the [convention] hall, the delegates had to travel four miles by special buses. Along the route, newly erected strips of brown wattle fencing failed to hide the ugliness they were supposed to disguise."

The Chain of Events

SATURDAY, AUGUST 24/SUNDAY, AUGUST 25
The tension was mounting the weekend before the convention began. One young man wrote in a letter to his girlfriend, "I realize at this time that there are very good chances that I may be injured or arrested because I am here. I believe that I along with many thousands more will be stopped from demonstrating our opposition to the war." On Saturday, in the afternoon, antiwar protesters gathered in Lincoln Park, located in Chicago's northern section. A curfew had been set for 11 PM, but by 10:30 about eight hundred people were still there. Mayor Daley's police force braced for a confrontation, but none occurred—when the curfew hour struck, everyone left peacefully. Protest leaders, however, had aggressive tactics planned for the following day.

Sunday, then, was when the real trouble started—at the same park, where about five thousand people had gathered to hear live music and participate in a "Festival of Life." But the festival got out of hand, and soon police and protesters were attacking each other. When the 11 PM curfew arrived, the crowd dispersed but police followed them, and more violence erupted. Also attacked were several members of the media (who were photographing and filming) and a few visiting dignitaries. The police, it seemed, were lashing out at everyone, and people were being beaten bloody and senseless. The aggression continued coming from both sides: police were attacking the protesters, many of whom were throwing stones and bottles, spitting on the police, and calling them names. Order wasn't restored until around 2 AM, and it wouldn't last long.

MONDAY, AUGUST 26

People began filtering back into the park early the next morning. All was quiet until two of the protest leaders were arrested and brought into custody. One political activist, Tom Hayden, had said earlier, "People have to be faced with the existential question of giving their life . . . forced into a moral squeeze, forced to decide whether they're [scared], asked what they are willing to do to stop the war." Word of the arrests spread quickly, and an angry crowd began to march toward the police station to demand the leaders' release. However, undercover agents had already reported this development, so the police were ready. The marching crowd was shocked to find officers surrounding the station, their weapons ready. They pleaded for the return of the two men, but to no avail. They considered more violent action, but ultimately decided against it.

Many of the protesters then gathered at nearby Grant Park, across the street from the Conrad Hilton Hotel, where many of the politicians participating in the convention were staying, along with members of the media. Since there were cameramen

Flag-waving activists swarm a statue during the Grant Park demonstration that took place in Chicago at the time of the Democratic National Convention.

and reporters on hand, the protesters saw an opportunity. A group split off to a nearby hill, where they swarmed a statue of Civil War general John Logan. In spite of the presence of reporters and cameramen, the police responded harshly, grabbing people and swinging their nightsticks. Eventually the crowd dispersed and the incident ended—but the mood between protesters and police had worsened.

Meanwhile, the convention officially began at Chicago's International Amphitheater, less than a mile away. Mayor Daley, knowing he was speaking not only to the thousands of Democrats but to the public at large, said he had every intention of keeping law and order and that the convention would not be interrupted by anyone. (Daley had also made it clear that he supported President Johnson's policies on the Vietnam War.) When the Democratic leadership began discussing the future of the party, tempers flared. Delegates from around the country hoped to keep Hubert Humphrey from securing the nomination, but they knew they were in the minority.

Late that evening tensions between protesters and police reached a flashpoint. Back in Lincoln Park the police arrived shortly after the 11 PM curfew and told everyone to leave the park. The officers were more nervous than on the previous night, having heard that some protesters now had weapons and were prepared to use them. Most people left without incident, but about a thousand defiantly remained. Shortly after midnight a police car nosed its way into the crowd and was immediately assaulted with rocks and bottles, which dented the body of the vehicle and smashed its windows.

The officers jumped out of the car and were joined by about three hundred others. Grenades filled with tear gas flew into the crowd of protesters, who scattered in every direction.

Police grabbed people almost randomly, beating them into submission. Protesters fought back whenever and however they could, but many lay unconscious as screams filled the air and ambulances came and went. Again, the media captured much of the chaos on film—and again, the police made no effort to exclude journalists from the violence. One reporter tried to persuade an officer not to strike him by showing his press credentials, but it didn't help. The rioting continued until the early hours of the morning.

TUESDAY, AUGUST 27

Media outlets around the country responded angrily to the news that their people were being attacked. They demanded an explanation from Mayor Daley and the police leadership. But Daley backed his officers, saying they were only doing what was necessary to maintain order. Meanwhile, protest leaders were complaining to every reporter they could find—they had a constitutional right to voice their opinions in public, even if those opinions were in direct opposition to those of the government. The police, they said, had no business trying to muzzle them. The media enthusiastically provided coverage of the protesters' activities in newspapers and on television.

There were only a few minor incidents during daylight hours. Most of the protesters were recovering from the mayhem of the previous night, some in hospital beds and emergency rooms. Protest leaders came out to speak to the crowds who were gathering as darkness fell. Black Panther chairman Bobby Seale stood in Lincoln Park and encouraged people to fight back against the police with whatever means were available—including anything that would work as a weapon. "If a [cop] comes up to us and starts swingin' a billyclub and you check around and you got your piece, you gotta down that [cop] in defense of yourself," he said at one point. His speech served to stir up more anger not only among the protesters but among law enforcement officials as well.

In Grant Park, across from the Conrad Hilton, a quieter gathering was taking place. It was so civil, in fact, that police eventually decided to lift the curfew in that area and allow the crowd to camp overnight. These protesters were less radical types: clean-cut young supporters of Senator McCarthy, middle-aged and middle-class professionals, members of pacifist organizations, and others. The police lingered nearby and kept watch, monitored in turn by a bank of television cameras, but extreme force was not used in Grant Park that night.

At the convention debate still raged over whether a quick end to the Vietnam War should be considered as part of Democratic Party policy. Since most party members supported President Johnson, they rejected the idea of an antiwar policy "plank." But others insisted that if the party was to have any chance of keeping the White House from the Republicans, the goal of a quick exit from Vietnam had to be part of their platform (the collection of policies and directives that elected officials would follow).

A large number of radical protesters decided to remain at Lincoln Park past the 11 PM curfew and stand their ground. But police had some surprises this time. Along with grenades, they had attached a canister of tear gas to a garbage truck and were blowing it out in a thick cloud. As protesters gagged and gasped for breath, law enforcement officials wearing protective masks stormed the area and began another round of violence. More shots were fired into the air, more blood ran from open wounds, and more arrests were made.

In the middle of the night, after most of the protesters had gone, the exhausted police force was replaced by about six hundred National Guard troops. In spite of being taunted and abused by remaining activists, the guardsmen took no action, and no further incidents of note occurred. But the rage on both sides was growing out of control now—and the worst was yet to come.

WEDNESDAY, AUGUST 28

As on the past two days the morning began quietly, with protesters arriving late, many still stung from the emotional and physical trials of the previous night. Rumors began circulating that a rally was to be held at Grant Park, in full view of the media cameras that had been set up across the street at the Hilton Hotel, followed by a march to the amphitheater where the convention was being held. Again, Tom Hayden provided some evocative words for both the protesters and the police—"This city and the military machinery it has aimed at us won't permit us to protest. Therefore we must move out of this park in groups throughout the city and turn this excited, overheated military machine against itself. Let's make sure that if blood is going to flow let it flow all over this city." Since this was the day when the delegates were going to vote on the nominees for the presidential ticket, Democratic protesters were determined to play a role in the process. If nothing else, they wanted their voices to be heard.

By midday police were everywhere. They handed out leaflets warning that a march to the amphitheater was illegal and would result in both arrests and a show of force. The protesters, now numbering about 13,000, were trying to figure out what to do—hold a rally in the park, ignore police warnings and march anyway, or perhaps try something else. Many of the activist leaders who had been around for the last few days were noticeably absent. Some had been arrested, a few were recovering from injuries, and others had left Chicago. But a few remained, trying desperately to focus the crowd with a plan of action.

The first of the day's violence began when a teenage boy tried to remove an American flag from one of the park's poles. Several police officers rushed over and stopped him. They were attacked by the crowd, who pelted them with rocks, cans, sticks, and balloons filled with tap water or urine. After the boy was removed, others continued lowering the flag, then raised up a red shirt in its place—symbolizing, among other things, the blood that was being spilled by young soldiers in Vietnam. More police arrived, and a vicious melee broke out. Some activist leaders, using microphones, pleaded for calm. Others, however, had run out of patience with the police's brutal tactics and urged the crowd to fight back.

The National Guard arrived on the scene with rifles, bayonets, grenade launchers, and machine guns—the kind of weaponry normally reserved for all-out warfare. Some of the troops were ordered to protect and block off all routes to the amphitheater, while others, along with the police, surrounded the protesters to keep them contained. The crowd eventually began breaking up, feeling there was no point in hanging around in the presence of so much security. But then word began drifting down that there were indeed several clear pathways to the amphitheater. Large portions of the formerly centralized crowd began wandering around, which worried the police and guardsmen. Eventually about seven thousand protestors ended up at the intersection of Jackson Street and Michigan Avenue. Several journalists also arrived in trucks and vans, with their cameras rolling. Soon reinforcement police streamed into the area, chanting, "Kill! Kill! Kill!" and protesters, knowing that the violence was being broadcast throughout the nation, responded with a chant of their own: "The whole world is watching . . . the whole world is watching."

Around 7:30 PM, police told protestors that the crowd had to break up and leave. Some obeyed, others hesitated. Then it began — taunted to the breaking point by protesters,

Taunted by protestors, Chicago's police go on the attack outside the Conrad Hilton Hotel in Chicago.

some police officers attacked viciously, delivering repeated blows with clubs and fists. Many of the protesters, feeling equally enraged and out of patience, fought back vigorously. Single policeofficers who found themselves surrounded by large groups struck out with sticks, rocks, and other objects. Police sprayed pepper spray in the protestors' faces, and some activists responded with sprays of their own. More officers arrived on the scene and, driven almost to madness by the sight of their injured brethren, launched fresh attacks. People were thrown through windows, run over by motor-cycles, and pinned against cars and walls. And all of this, plus much more, was being watched on television sets all across the country.

Eventually the crowd dispersed, but the protestors were far from finished with their rioting. They tore through the streets, setting fires, breaking windows in cars and buildings, setting off smoke and stink bombs, and attacking officers at random. More National Guard troops entered the area to restore order, but even with their considerable force and weaponry, the situation would remain out of hand for many hours to come.

At the convention, shortly after 11:00 PM, the nominating roll call began. Groups of delegates from all the states began casting their votes, and thousands of protesters in the streets and parks followed the progress on radio and television. It didn't take long to predict what the results would be — Hubert Humphrey was on his way to a landslide victory. This meant that the attempts by antiwar Democrats to include a "peace plank" in the party platform had been unsuccessful. The con-vention wouldn't formally end until late the following day — Thursday, August 29. But for the protesters, and millions of others, the crucial moment had come and gone. And as expected, Hubert Humphrey, now the official Democratic nominee, would stay loyal to President Johnson's stance on the most important issue of the day.

Reactions around the Country

The varied reaction to the 1968 Democratic Convention riots was astonishing. There wasn't even a uniform voice within the Chicago police department. One patrolman saw his role as nothing more than following orders. Even Superintendent James Conlisk said, "The force used was the force that was necessary," and he pointed out that no one had been killed. But another officer resignedly claimed that his and others' actions had little to do with police work. Deputy Attorney General Warren Christopher, present at the time, went further and said, "the Chicago Police there in front of the Conrad Hilton Hotel were utterly and completely out of the control of their superior officers."

Those who had learned of the riots but had not participated were also split. Radical liberals, incensed by the reaction of law enforcement officials, claimed that demonstrators merely engaging in peaceful protest—their constitutional right—had been attacked for doing so. They also said the police tried to then cover up their atrocities by seeking out reporters eager to share developments with their audience. Conservatives, on the other hand, claimed that the police had been provoked and antagonized, that many acts of defiance had been preconceived (rather than spontaneous, as many said), and that news coverage was biased—giving the nation an inaccurate view of what had transpired.

The Real Convention Winner — Richard M. Nixon

If there was one message clearly transmitted to the American public as a result of the 1968 Democratic Convention, it was that the Democratic Party was in shambles. The first sign of trouble was the decision of the party's leader, President Johnson, not to run for reelection, a move that surprised many. When the remaining delegates did nothing but bicker for days before nominating a man who would unconditionally support the war, voters had seen enough. In the general election in November the people voted in Richard M. Nixon, the Republican candidate. Nixon, a former vice president (to Dwight D. Eisenhower), had lost the 1960 presidential race to John. F. Kennedy; many thought of him as a political has-been. But Nixon sensed an opportunity in the Democratic Party's meltdown, and he was right—he was elected in 1968, then again in 1972. Two years later he would resign in disgrace after being

caught up in the Watergate scandal. His role in the coverup of his administration's break-in to the Democratic Party's headquarters at the Watergate Hotel in Washington, D.C., would have resulted in impeachment if he had not left on his own. So, ironically, Nixon first capitalized on the fall of the Democratic Party, then, through his own dishonesty, helped revitalize it.

Those who had followed the television coverage seemed to agree. CBS received almost ten thousand letters in the weeks and months that followed—and about 90 percent of them criticized the network for the subjective manner in which it portrayed the riots. A poll revealed that almost two-thirds of respondents felt Mayor Daley and the police had acted in an acceptable fashion. And of those who disapproved of the war, half still felt negatively toward the behavior of the rioters.

When all was said and done, the Democratic Party would pay a heavy price for the convention riots—Hubert Humphrey lost the election of 1968.

PART III:
AFTERMATH

WHAT HAS CHANGED SINCE, and as a result of, the riots of the 1960s? What have we learned? From all the anger, destruction, bloodshed, and death, have we extracted and utilized anything of value? Has society improved after all the sacrifice, darkness, and discord?

Positive Impact of the Riots

If there was one common thread uniting those who began in the 1960s to fight racial discrimination, the Vietnam War, intolerance toward homosexuals, subordinate treatment of women, and wholesale damage to the environment, it was the desire for *change*. People who felt that they and others were being denied equality by society's leaders wanted it known that the status quo was unacceptable.

That said, the rise in public awareness of these and other injustices was certainly one measurable improvement for which the social activism of the 1960s can proudly take credit. Before this period, many who were victims of discrimination were unheard, unseen, and therefore unknown. But never again — the severity of the rioting, if nothing else, made a clear

Social injustices have led to greater public awareness and the right to speak out against them.

statement: *We will not stand for this any longer.* The public at large was forced to take notice—and, for the first time, do something. Unfair treatment of minority groups became a topic of dinner-table conversation; the folly of the Vietnam War was discussed not just in government offices but in town meetings and classrooms. Passion stirred in the hearts of fair-minded individuals, many of whom became lawyers and businessmen and teachers. They were ready to contribute to the ongoing crusade for common decency. And those who had previously held these beliefs only in private were able to come forward and join others in working toward desired goals.

Another important result was the exposure of people who sought to sustain these unfair practices. Before the 1960s, many who knew discrimination was morally wrong were able to keep it alive simply because there was no force working against them. The social activism of the time changed all that—not only did the oppressed rise up, they also were able to shine a light on their oppressors for all the world to see. For example, police who regularly practiced brutal tactics without fear of reprisal knew they could now face serious consequences for their actions. The protests of the 1960s therefore had a powerful effect on the political process.

We are also more sensitive to the conditions that spark riots in the first place, and thus we're better able to avoid them. Civic leaders and their advisers can often see the pieces of a riot coming together, since they now have the benefit of experience. Similarly, the federal government passed antiriot legislation in the late 1960s, making the violent civil disturbances unlawful. Regardless of how much attention a riot brings to an important issue, it is only the radicals who *desire* collateral destruction. The riots teach us that crucial matters need to be discussed and resolved in a sensible manner. Why allow a situation to deteriorate until people feel the need to destroy entire communities? Rather than repair problems, this overly passive approach only creates more.

Negative Impact of the Riots

While some good did come from the riot-driven chaos, certain negatives cannot be discounted. The first and greatest, of course, was the cost in human life. Many died in the 1960s while battling for their causes. Most were healthy, idealistic, and young. How many families still grieve, all these years later, for the loss of those loved ones? How many tears have fallen? And all for the sake of injustices that should not have been allowed to flourish in the first place.

On a less personal note, the damage done to towns and cities is nearly inconceivable. Following the assassination of Martin Luther King Jr., there were riots in *hundreds* of cities. This caused millions of dollars to be spent repairing homes, businesses, vehicles, and so on — money that could have put toward bettering schools, roads, or health care. A city with a broken infrastructure, after all, can't function. How do you carry on daily life when there is no water, no food, no electricity, no safe place to sleep? Many of the riot-torn areas remained in a state of devastation for decades following the destructive events that had dragged them into the mire of ruin. Communities that had been building for generations were leveled in a matter of days. They became museums devoted to brief spells of madness that had disastrous long-term effects. Money stopped flowing in, right-minded citizens disappeared, and the rest of the world pretended not to notice. The unfortunate few who remained had to learn how to squeeze blood from stones. Crime increased, along with drug and alcohol use . . . and all from a few days past, when the citizens could keep their anger caged no longer.

It's also hard to ignore the damage that was done to the reputations of the people and organizations behind many of the riots. While it is true that ordinary citizens generally wish for the fair treatment of all people, it is also true that the public at large finds the act of rioting deplorable and unworthy of respect. To give rioters what they want is, in many people's minds, to give in to terrorism. One of the reasons King made such great progress for the black cause in his relatively short lifetime was his avowedly *nonviolent* approach—he would speak, he would march, he would argue, he would negotiate . . . but he would not destroy. Many of those who opposed him, disagreed with him, or even hated him still respected him. He was a builder, and builders usually are the people who get things done. The riots of the 1960s painted so many people as criminals that it was sometimes hard to recall what they were fighting for. In other words the *riots themselves* became a bigger issue than the reasons behind them. When that happened, many people were no longer able to take the participating groups seriously. They were felt to be too radical and dangerous, and thus their causes unworthy of consideration.

Thus, in regard to the racially motivated riots, the damage done to the civil rights movement was severe. Americans of all races felt that the extensive rioting of the 1960s harmed blacks the most. Polls taken among white Americans at the end of the decade suggested an increasingly negative attitude toward black citizens, not to mention all those in government who had empowered them. The election of Richard Nixon is one clear example of this — Nixon's political career had essentially ended in 1960, when he lost the presidential race to John F. Kennedy. But he shrewdly realized that he could use the fear generated by the riots nearly a decade later to make a comeback, taking political power away from the Democrats. He promised a return to a more lawful and orderly society, and the public, with images of Watts and the Chicago convention still fresh in their minds, went along. Many others in the Republican Party made sure the public's fear was constantly reinforced, giving the conservatives a power base that did not show serious signs of crumbling until the waning days of the administration of George W. Bush.

The Future

Recent history tells of riots that have occurred since 1968. In the year following the Democratic Convention there was another outbreak in Chicago. It lasted four days and, somewhat symbolically, started with a rally in Lincoln Park. In 1977 New York City suffered two days of rioting and looting after an electrical failure led to a citywide blackout. And in April 1992, nearly a week of violence resulted from the acquittal of four white Los Angeles police officers who had been charged with using unnecessary force against a black man after a high-speed car chase.

Nevertheless, rioting has occurred with diminishing frequency since the 1960s and 1970s. Is it because we as a society have learned from those horrors and made the necessary adjustments? Have we taken steps to minimize the probability of such incidents recurring? Surely anyone with common sense hopes that this is the case. It is always preferable to work through a problem in a calm and rational manner.

Conversely, a vicious and destructive approach to any issue rarely produces a favorable outcome. Most of the rioters of the 1960s simply wanted to be heard, to have a voice in the political process. This is one of the most invaluable elements of a free society, and when that element is discarded, anger begins to grow. That's usually where chaos begins—and we need to keep this awareness in mind at all times. Or, in the words of American philosopher and poet George Santayana, "Those who cannot remember the past are condemned to repeat it."

Timeline

1863 President Abraham Lincoln issues the Emancipation Proclamation, granting freedom to millions of slaves in America.

1954 The U.S. Supreme Court makes a unanimous landmark decision in *Brown v. Board of Education* that the segregation of black students from white students is unconstitutional.

1955 Rosa Parks refuses to give up her seat on a bus to a white man, prompting her arrest but also spurring the organization by Martin Luther King Jr. and others of the Montgomery bus boycott.

1964 A riot breaks out in July in the New York neighborhoods of Harlem and Bedford-Stuyvesant following the fatal shooting of a black teenager by a white police officer. On August 7 Congress votes to approve the Gulf of Tonkin Resolution, which gives President Lyndon B. Johnson broad powers in declaring and spearheading a war against North Vietnam. A riot breaks out on August 28 in Philadelphia following the arrest by two police officers, one black, the other white, of the black female driver of a car that had stalled.

1965 Operation Rolling Thunder, a massive bombing raid on North Vietnam, begins on President Johnson's orders. The first American troops hit the ground in Da Nang, Vietnam's fourth-largest city. A riot of massive proportions breaks out in the Watts area of Los Angeles following the routine traffic stop of two black men.

1968 The Tet Offensive, against U.S. and South Vietnamese forces, begins in Vietnam. Dr. Martin Luther King Jr. is assassinated on April 4 while standing on the balcony of the Lorraine Motel in Memphis, Tennessee. President Johnson signs the Civil Rights Act of 1968 on April 10, which includes, among other things, the Anti-Riot Act, making it unlawful to lead or incite crowds to destructive behavior. Antiwar protesters and police clash violently in Chicago, where the Democratic National Convention is being held on August 26 to 29.

Notes

Part I: Anger

p. 10, "The green sign on the Birmingham city buses . . .":
James Roberson, quoted in Ellen Levine, *Freedom's
Children: Young Civil Rights Activists Tell Their Own Stories.*
New York: Puffin Books, 1993, p. 6.

p. 10, "Campuses in the 1950s were not political places . . .":
William McConnell, *The Counterculture Movement of
the 1960s.* Farmington Hills, MI: Greenhaven Press,
2004, p. 34.

Chapter One

p. 15, "The slave . . . owes his labour to his master. . . .":
William John Grayson, "The Hireling and the Slave."
Charleston, SC: McCarter & Company, 1856.

p. 15, "You say it is unconstitutional—I think differently.":
Abraham Lincoln, in a letter to James Conkling,
August, 1863.

p. 20, "Second emancipation proclamation.": quoted in
Michael W. Flamm and David Steigerwald, *Debating the
1960s: Liberal, Conservative, and Radical Perspectives.* Lanham,
MD: Rowman and Littlefield, 2008, p. 132.

p. 24, "At the time the boycott began, . . .": Fred Taylor,
quoted in Levine, p. 29.

Chapter Two

p. 28, "You have brought to your great task of organizing
your country . . .": Dwight D. Eishenhower, quoted in

Tom Pendergast, *Defining Moments: The Vietnam War*.
Griswold, MI: Omnigraphics, Inc., 2007, p. 26.

p. 28, "We still seek no wider war.": Lyndon B. Johnson,
quoted in Fred R. Shapiro, ed., *The Yale Book of Quotations*.
New Haven, CT: Yale University Press, 2006.

p. 31, "My solution to the problem would be to tell the
North Vietnamese . . .": Curtis LeMay, *Mission with
LeMay*. New York: Doubleday, 1965.

p. 33, "We march to dramatize the world wide hope . . .":
National Mobilization Committee to End the War
in Vietnam, David Farber, *Chicago '68*. Chicago: The
University of Chicago Press, 1988, p. 69.

p. 35, "light at the end of the tunnel.": Johnson, quoted in
Pendergast, p. 105.

Chapter Three

p. 36, "The problem lay buried, unspoken . . .": Betty Friedan,
The Feminine Mystique. New York: Norton, 1963.

p. 41, "During the past quarter century this power has
not only increased to one of disturbing magnitude. . .":
Rachel Carson, *Silent Spring*. Boston: Houghton Mifflin,
1962.

p. 43, "Any criminal, infamous, dishonest, immoral,
or notoriously disgraceful conduct . . .": Federal
Executive Order 10450, April 27, 1953. http://www.
archives.gov/federal-register/codification/executive-
order/10450.html.

Chapter Four

p. 50, "Between the end of World war II and the early
1960s, . . .": Janet L. Abu-Lughod, *Race, Space, and Riots
in Chicago, New York, and Los Angeles*. New York: Oxford
University Press, 2007, p. 159.

p. 51, "I was threatened by a group of Negroes . . .":
Fred C. Shapiro, "The Talk of the Town: Bedford-
Stuyvesant." *The New Yorker*, August 1, 1964, p. 23.

p. 55, "Rumor spread along Columbia Avenue and its
environs . . .": Gerald Early, "No Other Life." http://
www.upenn.edu/gazette/0301/early.html.

p. 56, "A few years ago, a black lawyer told me . . .": Gerald
Early, "No Other Life."

p. 58, "We got a couple of calls from people stating that
something is happening . . .": Betty Pleasant, "Eyewitness
Accounts of the Watts Riots," *Los Angeles Wave* online —
http://www.wavenewspapers.com/default.asp?sourceid
=&smenu=71&twindow=&mad=&sdetail=4048&wpage
=1&s%20keyword=&sidate=&ccat=&ccatm=&restate=
&restatus=&reoption=&retype=&repmin=&repmax=&-
rebed=&rebath=%20&subname=, August 3, 2005.

p. 62, "After a thorough examination, the Commission has
concluded. . .": *A Report by the Governor's Commission on
the Los Angeles Riots*, December 2, 1965.

p. 64, "I heard a friend of mine say 'Hey, . . .'" :quoted
in Michael Flamm, *Law and Order: Street Crime, Civil*

Unrest, and the Crisis of Liberalism in the 1960s. New York: Columbia University Press, 2005, p. 90.

Chapter Five

p. 67, "When we heard he was shot, everybody was devastated.": Thelma Eubanks, quoted in Levine, p. 139.

p. 70, "The day Martin Luther King was killed. . . .": Arlam Carrin, quoted in Levine, p. 140.

p. 71, "That Monday after the Rev. Martin Luther King Jr.'s murder. . .": Larry Carson, "When Baltimore Erupted in Rage," *The Baltimore Sun* online— http:// www.baltimoresun.com/news/opinion/oped/bal-op. riot04apr04,0,1391407.story, April 4, 2008.

p. 73, "It was like total chaos. People running and screaming . . .": Reginald Kelly, quoted in Joe Holley, "More Recollections of DC Riots Following King's Death," *The Washington Post* online— http://www. washingtonpost.com/wp-dyn/content/article/2008/04/06/ AR2008040602110_pf.html, April 6, 2008.

p. 76, "I sat in my driver's seat, overwhelmed by emotions . . .": Larry Aaronson, quoted in Holley, "More Recollections of DC Riots Following King's Death," April 6, 2008.

p. 79, "I said to him very emphatically . . .": Richard J. Doley, quoted in Farber, p. 145.

Chapter Six

p. 85, "No matter what we do, the Mobilization and other organizations . . .": Roger Wilkins, quoted in Farber, p. 156.

p. 86, "Hey, hey, LBJ . . .": Walter LaFeber, *The Deadly Bet*. Oxford: Rowman and Littlefield, 2005, p. 50.

p. 88, "What is new, and what is very much a product of the Administration's single-minded preoccupation . . .": Eugene McCarthy, *Eugene McCarthy on the Issues*. San Francisco: San Francisco McCarthy for President Campaign Research Bureau, 1968, p. 22.

p. 89, "To reach the [convention] hall . . .": quoted in LaFeber, p. 50.

p. 89, "I realize at this time . . .": quoted in Farber, p. 165.

p. 90, "People have to be faced with the existential question of giving their life . . .": Tom Hayden, quoted in Farber, p. 183.

p. 93, "If Bobby Seale, comes up to us and starts swingin' a billy club . . . ": quoted in Farber p. 190.

p. 95, "This city and the military machinery it has aimed at us . . .": Hayden, quoted in Farber, p. 196.

p. 99, "The force used was the force that was necessary.": James Conlisk, quoted in Flamm, p. 158.

p. 99, " . . . the Chicago police there in front of the Conrad Hilton Hotel . . .": Warren Christopher, quoted in Flamm, p. 158.

Part III: Aftermath

p. 109, "Those who cannot remember the past . . .": George Santayana, *The Life of Reason*. New York: Charles Scribner's, 1905, p. 284.

Further Information

Books

Caputo, Philip. *10,000 Days of Thunder: A History of the Vietnam War.* New York: Atheneum Books, 2005.

Gold, Susan Dudley. *Lyndon B. Johnson.* New York: Marshall Cavendish Benchmark, 2009.

McNeese, Tim. *The Civil Rights Movement: Striving for Justice* (Reform Movements in American History). New York: Chelsea House, 2007.

O'Connell, Kim A. *Primary Source Accounts of the Vietnam War* (America's Wars through Primary Sources). Berkeley Heights, NJ: Enslow, 2006.

Stokes, John A., and Herman Viola. *Students on Strike: Jim Crow, Civil Rights, Brown, and Me.* Washington, DC: National Geographic School Publishing, 2007.

Various authors. Civil Rights Movement series. Greensboro, NC: Morgan Reynolds, 2006–present.

DVDs

The History Channel Presents: Voices of Civil Rights. Featuring Dr. Martin Luther King, Jr. A&E Home Video, 2006.

Vietnam War Secrets. BCI / Eclipse, 2007.

Vietnam War with Walter Cronkite. Featuring veteran newsman Walter Cronkite. CBS News Video Library, 2008.

Websites

NAACP

http://www.naacp.org/
Home page of the National Association for the Advancement of Colored People.

The Sixties

http://www.pbs.org/opb/thesixties/
A website concerning the 1960s.

The Vietnam War

http://www.vietnamwar.com/
Well-organized and content-rich site that calls itself the Ultimate Resource for the Vietnam War.

American Studies

http://www.colorado.edu/AmStudies/lewis/2010/students.htm
Colorado University's page on the student movement and struggle for democracy in the 1960s.

Bibliography

Abu-Lughod, Janet L. *Race, Space, and Riots in Chicago, New York, and Los Angeles*. New York: Oxford University Press, 2007.

Carson, Larry. "When Baltimore Erupted in Rage." *The Baltimore Sun* online: April 4, 2008. http://www.baltimore sun.com/news/opinion/oped/bal-op.riot04apr04,0,1391407 .story.

Carson, Rachel. *Silent Spring*. New York: Houghton Mifflin, 1962.

Early, Gerald. "No Other Life." *The Pennsylvania Gazette*, March/April, 2001: 32–37.

Farber, David. *Chicago '68*. Chicago: The University of Chicago Press, 1988.

Flamm, Michael. *Law and Order: Street Crime, Civil Unrest, and the Crisis of Liberalism in the 1960s*. New York: Columbia University Press, 2005.

Flamm, Michael W., and David Steigerwald. *Debating the 1960s: Liberal, Conservative, and Radical Perspectives*. Lanham, MD: Rowman & Littlefield, 2008.

Fogelson, Robert M. *The Los Angeles Riots*. New York: Beaufort Books, 1969.

Friedan, Betty. *The Feminine Mystique*. New York: W.W. Norton and Company, Inc., 1963.

Grayson, William John. *The Hireling and the Slave*. Charleston, SC: McCarter & Company, 1856.

Holley, Joe. "More Recollections of DC Riots Following King's Death." *The Washington Post* online: April 6, 2008. http://www. washingtonpost.com/wp-dyn/content/article/2008/04/06/ AR2008040602110_pf.html.

LaFeber, Walter. *The Deadly Bet*. Oxford, UK: Rowman & Littlefield, 2005.

LeMay, Curtis. *Mission with LeMay*. New York: Doubleday, 1965.

Levine, Ellen. *Freedom's Children: Young Civil Rights Activists Tell Their Own Stories*. New York: Puffin Books, 1993.

McCarthy, Eugene. *Eugene McCarthy on the Issues*. San Francisco: San Franciso McCarthy for President Campaign Research Bureau, 1968.

McCone, John A. (Chairman). *A Report by the Governor's Commission on the Los Angeles Riots*. Los Angeles: State of California, 1965.

McConnell, William, ed. *The Counterculture Movement of the 1960s*. Farmington Hills, MI: Greenhaven Press, 2004.

McWilliams, John C. *The 1960s Cultural Revolution*. Westport, CT: Greenwood Press, 2000.

Newman, Mark. *The Civil Rights Movement*. Edinburgh: Edinburgh University Press Ltd., 2004.

Office of the Federal Register, United States Government. "Executive Order 10450 — Security requirements for Government employment." The National Archives online. http://www.archives.gov/federal-register/codification/executive-order/10450.html.

Pendergast, Tom. *Defining Moments: The Vietnam War*. Griswold, MI: Omnigraphics, Inc., 2007.

Pleasant, Betty. "Eyewitness Accounts of the Watts Riots." *Los Angeles Wave* online: August 3, 2005. http://www.wavenewspapers.com/default.asp?sourceid=&smenu=71&twindow=&mad=&sdetail=4048&wpage=1&

s%20keyword=&sidate=&ccat=&ccatm=&restate=&
restatus=&reoption=&retype=&repmin=&repmax=&-
rebed=&rebath=%20&subname=.

Santayana, George. *The Life of Reason: Reason in Common Sense*. New York: Scribner's, 1905.

Shapiro, Fred C. "The Talk of the Town: Bedford-Stuyvesant." *The New Yorker*, August 1, 1964: p. 23.

Shapiro, Fred R, ed. *The Yale Book of Quotations*. New Haven, CT: Yale University Press, 2006.

Index

About the Author

WIL MARA is an award-winning novelist and author of more than eighty-five books. He has written many educational titles for young readers, covering subjects such as history, geography, sports, science, and nature, plus several biographies. More information about his work can be found at www.wilmara.com.